APOPTOSIS OF A NATION:

Environmental Intoxication and the Prevalence of HCV-4b Among the Dispossessed of Egypt

APOPTOSIS OF A NATION:
Environmental Intoxication and the Prevalence of HCV-4b Among the Dispossessed of Egypt

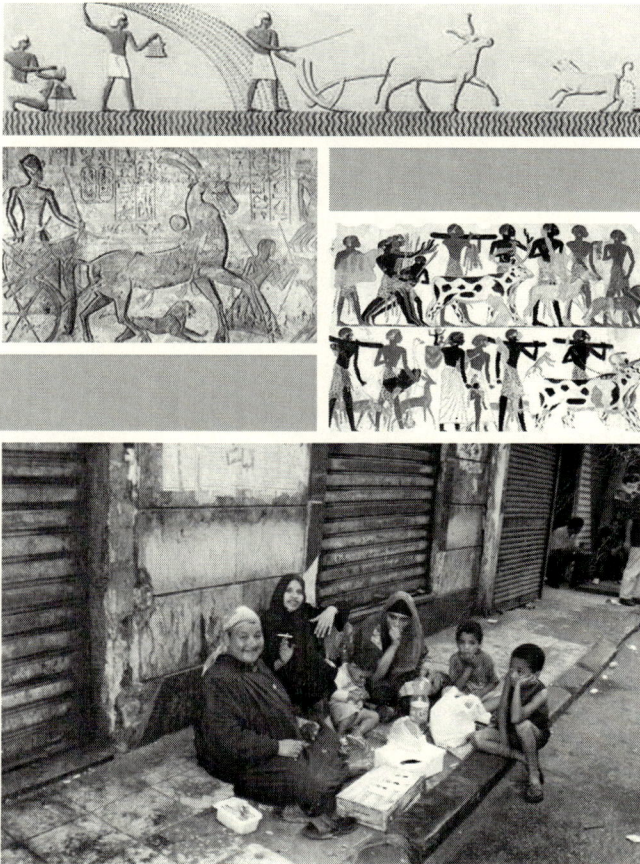

J.H. Wassili and Cyril Baradaeus

Submission date: 01/24/2012

Rev. date: 10/30/2013

To order additional copies of this book, contact:
Xlibris LLC
1-888-795-4274
www.Xlibris.com
Orders@Xlibris.com
111335

In many hundreds of books, pictures of Nazi victims rightly so were published so that humans will never ever forget the crimes committed during the dark years of 1938-1945. We should not forget the crimes committed against innocent Egyptians during the regimes of the 1952 colonels—Nasser, Sadat, and Mubarak—and the tailored alternative 2012. Considering the ruthlessness of the current political milieu together with their volatile instincts and cultural and political fabric, it is mandatory to safeguard the remnants of Egyptian scientists and secular intellectuals to salvage 7,000 years of culture.

The Glory and the Freshness of a Dream

Mena Daniel, Dr. Farag Fouda and Khaled Saed

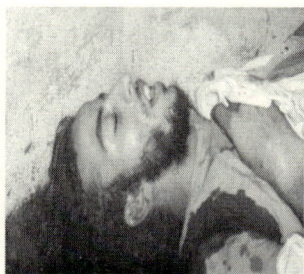  

October 9th 2011   June 8th 1992   June 6th 2010

```
What though the radiance which was once so bright
        Be now for ever taken from my sight,
      Though nothing can bring back the hour
 Of splendour in the grass, of glory in the flower;
        We will grieve not, rather find
        Strength in what remains behind;
            In the primal sympathy
        Which having been must ever be;
      In the soothing thoughts that spring
            Out of human suffering;
     In the faith that looks through death,
   In years that bring the philosophic mind.
```

William Wordsworth

Acknowledgment

To my parents, who instilled the precious commodity of free and uninhibited thinking in me, and my childhood friends who were mercilessly sacrificed, had their lives prematurely terminated, and their blood wasted in the heat of the Sinai desert in 1956, 1967, and 1973 on account of the 1952 coup officers' megalomania. The monumental task of the Egyptian philanthropist Mr. Naguib Sawires and Sir Dr. Magdi Yacoub to ease the burden of the very many with traumatic heart disorders and hepatic end-stage diseases is greatly acknowledged as well. The publication of this book would have not been possible without the unceasing support of Ms. M. Gomez, Ms. Kay Benavides, and Mr. E. Taylor as well the dedicated support of and Mr. K. Barnes is most appreciated.

Note

Upon request, supplementing materials to Egyptian newspaper articles are available at <authors.WB@gmail.com>

Abbreviations

Acute-phase response (APR); alanine aminotransferase (ALT); aspartate aminotransferase (AST);

albumin (Alb), pre-albumin (pre-Alb), haptoglobin (Hp); α-1-acid glycoprotein (AGP); C-reactive proteins (CRP); fibrinogen (Fb); transferrin (TF); α-1-antitrypsin (At);

cerebrospinal, peritoneal, and synovial fluid (CSF, PF, and SF respectively);

cholesterol (CHO); glucose (Glu); uric acid (UA); triacylglycerol (TG); α-fetoprotein (α-FP);

2-dimensional immunoelectrophoresis (2D-IEP); 2-dimensional electrophoresis (2D-EP);

erectile dysfunction (ED); sexual dysfunction (SD); nitric oxide (NO); cyclic guanosine monophosphate (cGMP); phosphodiesterase type 5 (PDE5);

Helicobacter pylori (*HBP*); hepatitis A, B, and C virus (HAV, HBV, and HCV respectively); human immunodeficiency virus (HIV); Yoshida sarcoma (YS);

hypothalamic-pituitary-adrenal axis (HPA); thyrotropin-releasing hormone (TRH); thyroid-stimulating hormone (TSH); triiodothyronine (T3); thyroxine (T4); coronary heart disease (CHD);

intraperitoneal (IP); intravenously (IV); mitochondrial-lysosomal (ML); and pelvic nerve electrical stimulation (PNES).

General Summary

Egypt, whose soil germinated the first civilization, monotheism, refined ethics, the culture of sharing the abundance of extracted natural resources, etc., among its populace, became the crucible of organic, moral maladies and the prime exporter of mutated bacterial and viral diseases. The enigma is these mutations are synchronized by several factors, namely, failing medical health (if there is any), abundant filth, cultural bankruptcy, overpopulation, dogmatic militarism, societal deprivation and characterization, etc. These domineering ingredients fossilized Egypt as of the 1952 coup in an irrevocable national apoptosis, thus threatening the integrity of other nations by the facile transfer of mutated diseases via frequent and cheap air travel. Therefore, it is deemed essential to elaborate on pollution and psychosis-induced organic maladies and grievous crimes evoked by dogmatic cults at the breeding sources, ghettos, and sporadic locations of the homeless in major cities and Upper Egyptian villages. The crippled social justice and imbalanced distribution of wealth among Egyptians are expected to accelerate the rate of bacterial and viral evolution, thus precipitating *de novo* medical risks as mutated species are resistant to known medical managements. Threat of mutated pathogens is twofold: (a) it could labor corrosive plagues to the precariously maintained social fabric of the Middle Eastern countries that is uniquely classifying and characterizing citizens according to their dogmatic affiliation, and (b) it would definitely compromise the integrity of the expensively managed medical care system of developed Western countries.

Ease of intercontinental ferrying of tropical diseases is well documented. For example, troops' marching during World War I is visualized as the causative factor of Spanish influenza, the lethal epidemic of 1918. Within a period of ten months, 22-40 million perished. Death in the USA was ~675,000 while ~22 million became ill. Victims were old individuals, children, and the feeblest. Similarly, HCV was imported into the USA by a few American soldiers who served in Vietnam (http://www.itmonline.org/arts/hepcstrat. htm). That is, regardless of the back-of-the-envelope justifications of military interventions in spots with hostile climatic conditions, such as Afghanistan, Somalia, Iraq, Sudan, Egypt, etc., politicians ought to consider one of the very many negative side effects, that is, the facilitation of cross-border transition of *de novo* genotypes of bacterial and viral diseases into Europe and North America proper with returning army personnel. An example of travel-facilitated migration of pathogens with visitors is on February 2,

2001. While en route to Hamilton, an African lady who landed in Toronto Air Canada 735 became seriously ill, suffering from an unknown illness, ebola virus? Another example is enterohemorrhagic *E. coli* (EHEC) bacterial transmission via fecal-oral route, eating undercooked and/or contaminated ground beef, swimming in or drinking contaminated water, and eating contaminated vegetables. Most recently, following the recent outbreak of EHEC in Germany, ten Swedes fell brutally ill and many more suffered other effects of the said bacterial infection. In this context, tests showed the municipal water supply of the city Östersund to embrace the same bacteria that precipitated the recent outbreak in Germany. *E. coli* O157:H7 can naturally be found in the intestinal contents of some cattle. Ruminants lack a receptor for the toxin produced by said bacteria; therefore, it does not affect them and is considered commensal. If, as suggested, contaminated vegetables imported from Spain were the vehicle of the *E. coli* outbreak in Germany, the relevant question remains why the intensity of the outbreak in Spain did not match that of Germany, with 1:520 cases and 0:11 mortalities respectively (http://thirteenthmonkey.blogspot.com/2011/06/e-coli-bioweapon-germany-updated.html). Was the German *E. coli* intentionally imported into/and or exported to Germany? Blaming Spanish cucumbers for the outbreak of *E. coli* into Germany proper is rather ridiculous indeed. However, it serves as an acceptable political maneuver to avoid unsettling the populace to the possibility of intentional export/import of *E. coli*. Interestingly, *E. coli* serotype O157:H7 is a *Gram-negative*, rod-shaped bacterium; a close mutant relative, the *Escherichia coli* O104:H4, is a rare enterohemorrhagic strain of the bacterium *Escherichia coli* and the cause of the 2011 *Escherichia coli O104:H4* outbreak.

Furthermore, incidents of individuals contracting meningitis in the cold, below 0°C Alberta, Canada's winter, to the south of the continent in humid-hot Louisiana, 40d incubation period of meningitis to show its symptoms in US individuals *versus* 2-3d incubation to manifest within inhabitants of tropical climates, and mosquito-transmitted West Nile virus in New York are examples of the ease of a pathogen's evolution to accommodate locations of radical climatic conditions. We are not preaching doomsday, but debating the genesis of health threats to occupants of the Western civilization and a collective means of erasing these threats at the breeding sites. It has also been reported, Swedish Easter eggs may contain slaughterhouse waste, e.g., gelatin from pigs and crushed insects. Dengue fever is exponentially contracted by Swedes as well. In 2010, 151 cases of the disease were reported by those returning from foreign trips, up from 100 the previous year. Infected individuals discovered the symptoms on their return, with about half of all cases picked up from trips to Thailand. Usually, the disease is carried by the mosquito *Aedes aegypti*. Although the mosquito originated in Africa, it is now found in tropical and subtropical regions throughout the world.

This book embodies conclusions of 10-year labor in Egypt, elaborating on (a) the prevalence of antibodies to HCV, HBV, malaria, *HBP*, HIV, and syphilis in serum of the disadvantaged living in substandard ghettos in major Egyptian cities and Upper Egypt; (b) an animal model and clinical data suggesting immune-rejection mechanisms for the expiry of patients with end-stage cirrhosis; (c) the $60\pm10\%$ decrease of plasma proteins in circulation of individuals with late HCV-renal failure, which modestly climaxed $20\pm5\%$ when said patients subsisted for 1 month while remaining in the sanitary milieu of the hospital on amino acids and carbohydrate-vegetarian diets enriched with 5% freeze-dried bovine colostrum, acetyl-L-carnitine, stevia in lieu of glucose, and 0.5 g silymarin; (d) the possible mutation of HCV-4b into a new subtype as 2 patients showed typical end-stage HCV liver cirrhosis whose peritoneal fluid had a parallel spectrum of organic and enzymatic activities to serum of end-stage HCV cirrhosis (nonetheless, assays for HCV antibodies in serum gave faint coloration); and (e) feasibility of redrawing the board of medical management of the poverty-stricken Egyptian populace plagued with HCV-4b: we are suggesting the development of a viable, noninvasive, economically affordable, and less agonizing technique, that is to replace serum of HCV-4b patients with synthetic substitutes in lieu of hepatic dialysis and/or liver transplant.

According to our research labor, it is our contention:

1. With the help of specialized receptors, some animals have evolved a sensory capacity to detect naturally occurring electric fields in the microvolt or even nanovolt range. The electric signals, which convey information about the structure of the environment and the activity of other animals, are processed in specific regions of the brain. When the use of other senses is limited because of darkness, murky water,

etc., animals manipulate this passive electric sense in navigational maneuverings, obstacle avoidance, or prey detection. During the course of evolution, some fish were assembled to embody an active electric sense (i.e., with the help of an electric organ), and specific electric fields were generated for communications or for pulsating a stronger electric wave to stun a prey. In humans, evolution of different and more complicated sensory functions may have turned these electric sensory capabilities redundant. Nonetheless, it is tempting to assume this functionality mutated to acquire the task of specific signals' transudation from the monitoring DNA pool to commence or to terminate a given biological process. Most likely, the specificity of particular signals designed to trigger given organic processes are proportional to and tailored to suit average surface-charge densities of corresponding lipid chips. Distribution of surface-charge densities of lipids are drawn according to meticulous arrangements of saturated, mono—and polyunsaturated fatty acids with various chain lengths on glycerol's backbone. Thus, lipids of specific locations are the cornerstones to timely accommodate or transude adequate electric charges proportional to given biological stimulatory processes.

Thus, interpretations of mechanisms of evoking and/or terminating hepatic inflammatory injuries leading to necrosis in terms of detailed organic structure of triacyl, diacylglycerols, and free fatty acids of adipose tissues of inflamed organs or contained in serum and other body fluids should be feasible. In this context, GLC spectral details of organic structure of triacyl and diacylglycerols of serum and body fluids are expected to mirror cytosolic and membrane lipids of cellular components of the inflamed organ. That is, detailed lipid analyses of serum or body lipids could be a viable candidate for monitoring pathological or psychological injuries and their regression on medical intervention. On the other hand, it is possible to relate organic structural changes of triacyl and diacylglycerols in serum and hepatic tissue lipids of inflamed individuals with activity of pancreatic phospholipase A2 in terms of the rate of lipolysis and buildup of inflammatory mediators (e.g., leukotrienes and prostaglandins), decoding of APR signals, and possible regression upon cessation of provoking stimulants. In this context, our explanatory GLC assays, using Rtx-65TC-fused silica column of lipids extracted from different tissues of animals (rabbit, bovine, hog, lamb, and buffalo) and birds (chicken and duck) revealed that (a) animals and birds have specific fingerprints of triacylglycerols with modifications in abundance of various triacylglycerols and elution time proportional to molecular weights and fatty acids saturation/ unsaturation (e.g., regardless of species, cardiac and kidney-collected lipids showed elevated abundance of saturated and higher molecular weight triacylglycerols *vis-à-vis* lipids extracted from intestinal adipose tissues), and (b) our initial observations suggest quantitative alterations in elution pattern and abundance of triacylglycerol fingerprints to severity and duration of various experimental inflammation, for example, inflection of diabetes, cirrhosis, and combined inflammation into experimental animals (data and interpretations will be published in due course).

2. Logically, since APR-signal transudation precedes organic release of IL-1, IL-6, TNF-α, etc., to precipitate an array of defensive mechanisms of APR changes, it should be possible to imitate these signals to stimulate the said APR without the necessity of the administered injurious stimuli. This is to counter (I) regeneration of remnants of surgically excised tumours, and (II) bacterial or viral insult and to abrogate it when necessary *without* administering steroidal or other anti-inflammatory agents, that is, eventual drug-free deprogramming of ailing signals, inducing hepatic inflammation.

3. The first tetrapods evolved from their aquatic ancestors, undergoing many structural and functional modifications. Limbs developed from lobe fins presumably to allow terrestrial locomotion, and this involved bone lengthening and musculature modification. Fish evolved into *amphibians, amphibians* into primates, and primates into man. Our preliminary GLC assay agrees with the above conclusion, thus documenting a similarity of certain high molecular weight saturated triacylglycerols of body adipose tissue and abdominal fat of wild catfish with that of rodents such as rats, lizards, and rabbits.

4. The supposedly flawless evolutionary process is believed to have attained the ultimate (i.e., yielding a perfect model as the end product) man/ woman for the sake of preservation of species. In healthy males, sperms are assembled and released at males' whims regardless of their age

while females are born with a specific number of ova, released once per month. It is medically established that the biological integrity of stored ova deteriorates as females advance in age with the concomitant risk of delivering genetically deformed infants. A closer scrutiny of the fragility of males' reproductive machinery to exposure to environmental toxins such as pesticides, mycotoxins, etc., is indicative that males' sex faculty has reached its optimal evolution and is declining. As every new life is a mutation of the previous, unless it is a perfect clone, it is feasible to suggest female gender is possibly in evolution to the immaculate ideal of releasing an ovum whenever mating is necessary *versus* the menstrual cycle, which ovulates a predetermined number of ova. Thus, it saves energy expenditure required to rebuild the endometrium at every fertility cycle and minimizes the vulnerability of the ova's chromatin to problems of division and breakage. Eventually, fetuses and infants of older mothers would have lesser probabilities of chromosomal abnormalities. This hypothetical female in active evolution increases the possibility of continuation of our species with greater chances of survival and/or adaptation to the current unfavorable intoxication of the environment.

5. Nature's evolutionary leaps into consorting humans' organic and psychological domains to geographical milieu advanced according to a strict DNA-like mapping with a rate limited to the laws of thermodynamics of maximal efficiency with minimal expenditure of energy. This is to elevate or to demote a populace of a given location with the lowest possible entropy of activation ΔS. Thus, characteristics of a population in terms of cultural achievements, extraction of wealth from nature, and ethics of distribution of extracted wealth among occupants of a location, à *la* tailored or natural laws, are naturally engraved into masses' particular genome, embracing the entirety of their cultural information. According to the same chain of thoughts, nature may be engraved in as many independent DNA compartments as many early tribes inhabited different continental locations. Albeit current ease of transportation allowed intracompartmental seepage of individuals, DNA characteristics of aliens remain recessed to readily manifest themselves at the opportune circumstance. That is, the nature-DNA engraving of individuals of a given tribe remains the rate-limiting step of their collective behavior, regardless of temporal changes such as

sudden wealth or communal decline, as in poverty-induced cultural decadence. Long-term intracompartmental communications of potentially different tribes may blunt the edge of the advanced one. Quixotic self-protection from outsiders together with resentment of inferiority may impel few members of the less fortunate tribe to enclave themselves into narcissistic Freudian cocoons of the sayings of distant ancestors, thus metamorphosing into χρυσαλλίς pupa of irrational violence. Although education and round-the-table dialogue would not modify societal-DNA differences, it may temper and dilute the impact of intracompartmental seepage *vis-à-vis* expensive and destructive wars.

> *There is no member of my body which is not the member of a god . . .*
> *Thoth protecteth my body altogether, and I am Ra day by day. I shall*
> *not be dragged back by my arms, and none shall lay violent hold*
> *upon my hands. And shall do me hurt neither men, nor gods, nor*
> *the Spirit-souls, nor the dead, nor any man, nor any pat-spirit, nor*
> *any rekhit-spirit, nor any hememet-spirit.* (The Egyptian *Book of*
> *the Dead*)

6. Typical of a male-oriented society, disadvantaged Egyptian females are more prone to contract HCV as they carry the burden of daily life. In given locations, (a) females accounted for ~38% incidence of HCV together with ~95% positive malaria and α-FP in serum and 4 isolated cases of females with syphilis-like bacteria, and (b) one adult female who tested positive for syphilis-like bacteria in serum had ~25% of her offspring with ~50% atrophied brain. Alarmingly, ~11 and 5.6% of females aged 4-10 years old tested positive for HCV and HBV in serum respectively. In another location, 11.5% and 1.3% of adult males tested positive for HCV and HBV, of which 56% and 6% tested positive for the same antibodies in their seminal fluid respectively. Similarly, among 44% of HCV-positive pregnant females, 25% tested positive for HCV in colostrums. Nonetheless, all tested negative for HIV 1+2 and syphilis.

Introduction to the Anatomy of the Current Egyptian Population

The Only Thing Necessary for the Triumph of Evil is that Good Men Do Nothing

Edmund Burke (1729-1797)

The major drive of the current presentation is to bring the dilemma of the dispossessed Egyptians, tightly engaged in sporadic unhygienic enclaves within major Egyptian cities, to the attention of the scientific community. Thus, a multidisciplinary exchange of scholarly thoughts of scientists from different disciplines and of psychiatrists may help in articulating possible mechanisms (1) to medically manage the deteriorating health of the Egyptian homeless, (2) to mentally sanitize the psychological milieu of said populace, and (3) to distill ethical values and refined education into the 3rd generation of homeless youth.

To start with, general terms as *just society, sanitary conditions, health care*, etc., are alien to contemporary Egyptians and, in particular, to dwellers of Upper Egypt. In Cairo, populated by ~18 million, >1.7 million dispossessed are occupying two major ghettos, *ul-Makkaber* (city of the dead, necropolis, or el-Arafa whose founding dates to the Arab conquest of Egypt in AD 641) and *ul-Zabbaleen* (rubbish collectors), while others are cohabiting in sporadic enclaves within the city. All are barely living far below the medically accepted norm, if there is any. Unless medically and sanitarily overhauled, their milieu is the suitable environment to breed *de-novo* subtypes of bacterial and viral diseases, which could be transported within walking distances to cancerously inhabited downtown Cairo, Alexandria, or a few hours' flight to major European and North American locations by cheap air travel. In Western societies, the term *homeless* usually denotes elderly males and very few females. However, in Egypt, with long traditions of an ancient civilization characterized by healthy family bond and respect specifically when it comes to women and children, a great proportion of the current Egyptian homeless are women and 5-12 year-old children. It became a customary scene to encounter a begging woman accompanied by her 3-4 children. By comparison, the poetry of a deceased ancient Egyptian child, Thothrekh, son of Petosiris, the high priest of Thoth, manifests the agony and the deep attachments of the relations and peers to the dead child:

Who hears my speech, his heart will grieve for it,
For I am a small child snatched by force,
Abridged in years as an innocent one,
Snatched quickly as a little one,
Like a man carried off by sleep.
I was a youngster of 2 years
When taken to the city of eternity,
To the abode of the perfect souls;
I therefore reached the Lord of Gods,
Without having had my share.
I was rich in friends,
All the men of my town,
Not one of them could protect me!
All the town's people, men and women,
Lamented very greatly,
Because they saw what happened to me,
For they esteemed me much.
All my friends mourned for me,
Father and Mother implored Death;
My brothers, they were head-on-knee,
Since I reached this land of deprivation.

Ancient Egyptian Literature: Vol III: The Late Period.
Miriam Lichtheim

At the moment, 1,370 years later, both genders of Egyptian children are kidnapped, sexually assaulted, and murdered.[1] It is very obvious that tourism for the sole purpose of sex[2] has legalized violence against the dispossessed Egyptian females, especially frequent sex assaults committed by street gangs (viz., *Al Gomhuria*, March 1, **2009**). The consequences are very many illegitimately born and mismanaged children.[3] Because of the unripe ethics of the society, these infants will be abandoned in the streets; thus the dilemma would mushroom, or wild dogs and cats may interrupt this sequence of misery.[4]

These children are not only the initiating media for bacterial and viral mutation into *de novo* genotypes, but are also silent targets of sexual abuse, murder, and dogmatic rearing. The dilemma of the *Egyptian homeless,* according to our 10-year search, is a bewildering and an acutely perplexing mosaic of intricate societal, psychological, and environmental intoxication and medical factors. Impoverishment, deprivation, conflicting interest, and apparent apathy induced this abhorrent dilemma to proliferate the said sporadic enclaves of the dispossessed within every corner of a large Egyptian city. It is rather impossible to segregate the causative factors and to tackle each separately; therefore, we have to deal with this complex societal-medical problem as is. For example, the children of penniless families, not to mention the homeless, suffer from an array of organic and psychological ailments, for example, asthma, chronic bronchitis, HBV, HCV, cancer (many infants born with advanced hepatoma expired as of the 7th day of delivery), and sexual abuse by elderly peers and/or immediate relatives. Thus, the current societal-medical dilemma in Egypt is in symphony with the conclusion of Donohoe, associating environmental degradation and social injustice with the declining health of tormented communities.[5] Also, hot and arid climatic conditions, overpopulation, pollution, weather extremes of global warming, unsustainable agricultural and ill fishing practices together with overconsumption, prejudiced distribution of wealth, rise of the corrupt corporations, dogmatic militarization of the illiterates, and organized bias against women and minorities ultimately yield increased poverty, intolerance, flagrant abuse of human rights, overcrowding, famine, species loss, acute/chronic medical illnesses, and an increasingly unpredictable internal chaotic situation that prophesies Malthusian anarchy and disasters.[5] The Egyptians are feverishly nourishing the seeds of Malthusian anarchy and disasters; for example: according to dogmatic affiliations, the official bias was evident in (i) denying Mena Nashed, a handicapped blind child, the necessary rehabilitation care and (ii) the violation of human rights of laypersons as in the absurdity of arresting a Christian male for marrying a Muslim female. The irony is the homeless, happily congregated in mass in Tahrir Square, Cairo, Alexandria, and other cities, who were the recipients of free blankets, daily meals, etc., become the major factor behind the social turmoil climaxed by the departure of the regime. In other words, the homeless by-product of the 1952 coup managed to dismantle the causative factor, that is, the last officer in the 60-year-long dictatorial hold of daily life in Egypt, alas replacing them with different characters of the same school.

Therefore, it is deemed essential to scan the prevalence of tropical inflammatory threats among the occupants of these ghettos and other sporadic locations. Diagnoses of *HBP*, HCV, HBV, malaria, syphilis, HIV, etc., together with assays of the hepatic efficiency in terms of biosynthesis and release of serum proteins into circulation, were carried out. This is to monitor hepatic-induced APR to environmental toxins saturating their rubbish-scavenged diets and polluted air and drinking water and, finally, to comment on aberrations of their psychological realm. Besides *Schistosoma mansoni*, long-term bioaccumulation of aluminum, lead, mercury, hexavalent chromium, polychlorinated biphenyls, and lipophilic toxins, (e.g., aflatoxin B1, DDT, organophosphorus, and carbamate pesticides[6, 7]) are expected to induce initial sharp hepatic inflammatory APR, which turns into a muted response indicative of a consumed liver mass. This is not only a pivotal factor precipitating cardiac maladies, thus hastening the expiry of the dispossessed at a relatively young age, 42-47y, but possibly, this may also injure the DNA characterization to potentiate serious biologically inheritable familial DNA aberrations. In a location, ~38% of destitute adult females tested positive for HCV-4b, a hepatotropic RNA virus that often evades effective immune recognition and has a propensity to persist in the majority of acutely infected individuals, thus precipitating liver cirrhosis and hepatocellular carcinoma in 80% of carriers.[8] The origin of the HCV epidemic in Egypt is the corollary of several factors, for example, sharing needles and rusty surgical tools by private barber-doctors performing male circumcision and female mutilation, the 1960s intravenous schistosomiasis mismanagement, ignorant midwives assisting delivery of babies, illegitimate abortions, and hospital-acquired infection of immune-deficient patients with renal failure on long-term hemodialysis.[9,10] According to table 1 and presentations 1 and 2, the published statistical distribution of HCV among Egyptians suggests major cities such as Alexandria and Cairo have the least, 5.9% and 8.2% counts, respectively, of the ~22% national occurrences. The Nile Delta has the highest prevalence, ~28.4%. However, our detailed assays verified higher proportions of HCV-carriers in *ul-Makkaber* and *ul-Zabbaleen* ghettos and sporadic enclaves of homeless in Cairo, Alexandria, and Upper Egyptian villages. Most unsettling is our observation that 10-15% of HCV-positive <10y children were born to either parent or both parents with HCV RNA in circulation. In general, anti-HCV IgM and PCR-positive mothers are more likely to communicate HCV to their newly born infants. Furthermore, needle sharing by addicts, ~8.5% of the population, is a major contributing factor to the prevalence of HCV-4b among disfranchised Egyptian youth.[11] Egypt's National

Council for Fighting and Treating Addiction reported that ~439,000 children are regular drug users and ~12.2% of students are dependent on drugs, while 9% smoke bango, 3% prefer hashish, and 0.21% take heroin or chemical drugs. Although bango is the drug of choice, cocaine, heroin, methamphetamine, and ecstasy are also available in local markets. This may rationalize why the higher proportion of Gaza population, ones who are bordering Egypt, tested HCV-4b-positive. Logically, Gaza's location as a 2-hour drive to the mecca of science, the Weizmann Institute of Science, Rehovot, Israel, makes it an ideal combination to tackle possible managements of HCV-4b. Unfortunately, the political fabric of the strip is soaked into abundant theories of conspiracies and lunatic absurdities that would turn a Samaritan approach to medically relieve individuals acutely in contract with HCV-4b into futility and a waste of time. This creates a unique situation of a country hostage to the bio-terror of a lethally camouflaged medical threat at its borders that is communicable with daily migrant workers.

We are also reporting electrophoretic data authenticating substantial ($60 \pm 10\%$) depression of total serum proteins of end-stage HCV patients coupled with renal failure relative to controls. In this context, kinetics and mechanisms of biosynthesis and release of APR proteins induced by multi-inflammatory stimuli (e.g., environmental intoxications, bacterial lesions, hepatic viral infections, psychological lesions, etc.) proceeded according to a multi-inflammatory syndrome developed in animal models.

Discussion

In one location, 12.4% and 1.8% of the 5-25y male population tested positive for HCV and HBV respectively. Approximately 65% and 25% of infected mature males tested positive to the same antibodies in semen (table 2). Alarmingly, 40% of postpartum women tested positive for HCV, of which 50% tested positive for HCV antibodies in colostrum (table 2). In another location, 2.1% and 23% males and 6.3% and 38% females of the same age, >20-60y, tested positive for HBV and HCV infection respectively (table 3). By contrast, the prevalence of HCV and HBV in Korean population is 1% and 5%, respectively.[12] NH_4^+ in the serum of HCV and HBV Egyptian individuals fell within the healthy range symptomatic of an early stage of hepatic insult, while proportions of Glu, CHO, and TG seriously fell below those of healthy Canadians (table 3).

This phenomenon could be the ramifications of deprivation of healthy nutrients together with acquired maladies. Concomitantly, 2D-IEP of HCV or HBV-positive serum samples, against antihuman control serum proteins prepared in rabbits, showed $25 \pm 10\%$ reduction of total proteins relative to healthy Canadian controls. While 2D-IEP of HCV-positive serum against its antibodies developed in rabbits, it showed minor immunoprecipitates in the β-region, totaling 5%-7% of total proteins. This may suggest specific *de novo* biosynthesis and/or conditional catabolism of serum proteins, proportional to the insufficiency of the metabolically fatigued hepatocytes. On the other hand, 2D-IEP of plasma of early HCV-renal failure patients, collected postroutine of kidney dialysis, showed unorthodox APR spectrum of plasma proteins, that is, 10%-20% reduced Alb and pre-Alb and less-reduced AGP, Fb, TF, α-At, Hp, and CRP. At end-stage HCV renal insufficiency, 2D-IEP revealed a substantial $76 \pm 9\%$ decrease of Alb and pre-Alb. This is suggestive of metabolically fatigued hepatocytes whose pathways are dominated by catabolism of hepatic intracellular and serum proteins to provide an intracellular hepatic pool with essential carbohydrates and amino acid monomers. This is to maintain the primary hepatic function (i.e., biosynthesis and release of defensive APR plasma proteins) as viable as possible (table 4). Interestingly, 2D-IEP of HCV-renal failure patients' serum showed obvious deformation in proteins cascaded under albumin's immunoprecipitate in terms of electrophoretic mobility and width of peak. This is indicative of partially biosynthesized fragments or metabolites of albumin with different chemical structures and molecular weights proportional to the severity of the chronic inflammation. Therefore, a combination of perpetual hepatic inflammation induced by an etiological factor (HCV in diabetics) is an epitome of the precipitation of hepatocellular carcinoma[13], especially, without exception, HCV individuals who tested positive for α-FP in serum (table 3). According to national reporting, 14% of Egyptians are diabetic and 12% are en route to full manifestation of the disease.[14]

As mentioned above, a preliminary trial to provide end-stage HCV patients with renal failure with a better quality of life was carried out. These individuals, kept for a period of one month within the sanitary milieu of a specially built intensive care ward, were allowed to subsist on an aseptically prepared diet that was composed of partially hydrolyzed vegetarian ingredients with the essential range of amino acids and carbohydrates;

moreover, it was supplemented with 5% freeze-dried bovines' colostrum, 0.5 g silymarin, and acetyl-L-carnitine, a nutrient that helps the body turn fat into energy while substituting sugar with a natural ingredient, stevia. At the end of the trial, ~60% of these individuals regained a limited physical maneuverability together with 2D-immunoelectrophoretic precipitates of their serum proteins manifesting a modest elevation of $20\pm5\%$ in the percentages of various APR serum proteins. Thus, a controlled diet enriched with natural supplements has modestly decreased the metabolic load on fatigued hepatocytes, allowing partial restoration of the hepatic faculty pertaining to the biosynthesis and export of plasma proteins into circulation. That is, with the limited financial resources of the dispossessed Egyptians, calculated manipulation of diet is a viable and less stressful alternative to (i) the expensive combination of pegylated interferon α-2b and ribavirin, designed mainly to address HCV-1 and 2, not necessarily HCV-4b, and (ii) invasive liver transplant.

As expected, CSF, SF, PF, male semen fluid, and colostrum samples of HCV-positive females cross-reacted with anti-human plasma proteins showing a similar qualitative spectrum of APR immuneprecipitates. Also, our preliminary trials confirmed an indiscriminate cross-reaction of antibodies to colostrum and semen proteins developed in rabbits, with male and female serum proteins yielding *qualitative 2D-immunoprecipitates that were mirror images of those developed using human anti-serum proteins.* That is, bio-organics of semen, synovial, and colostrum fluid embraced an approximately similar protein/carbohydrate molecular core, however, with partial similarity of terminal determinants to those of filtered serum ingredients into the corresponding organ. Thus, testing positive for HCV antibodies in CSF, SF, and colostrum fluids collected from HCV patients is inevitable. Nonetheless, this observation does not dispense with the release and biosynthesis of functionally specific proteins to these locations in humans. Although this particular thesis is not the focus of our quest, that is, zeroing in on the efficient medical management of the dispossessed Egyptians, it is a subject of our intensive research. To top it, on the account of cohabitation with field animals (cows, donkeys, dogs, rodents, etc.), ~15% and 7% of HCV-positive male population of this particular site with renal failure showed positive cohabitation of HDV and HGV respectively in circulation (table 2). Additionally, 5% who tested positive for HCV showed HBV cohabiting their circulation.

Pesticides in Females' Colostrums

Without exception, all samples of collected colostrums contained halogenated chemicals, notably neurotoxic polychlorinated biphenyls, carcinogens as DDT, polybrominated diphenyl ethers, hexachlorobenzene, and surprisingly, 2,3,7,8-tetrachlorodibenzo-*p*-dioxin. Assayed colostrum samples embraced 7- to 9-fold the Canadian allowed limits in human or animal body fluids. The rationale for this excessive level of toxins in colostrums is women's habitation of agricultural communities that are abusing the utilization of imported in-bulk chemicals, which are repackaged/ sold to locals without labels detailing information pertaining to ingredients, limits of applications, and toxicity. As well the lack of collective measures to collect and recycle containers with residual chemicals scattered into open fields or the river Nile and/ or using them to carry home prepared drinks is adding to the problem of accumulated toxins into body fluids of tested individuals, particularly females and their newly born children.

Thus, toxins are transmitted into children from the moment of their incipience to breast-feeding age. Worse is the social imperative impelling children to accompany their parents to work in the fields at a tender age; thus, lipophilic toxins would exponentially bioaccumulate within their adipose tissues. Considering 1- to 5-year-old children consume >3 times more food per body weight than average adults do, besides precipitating other major side effects, bioaccumulated pesticides induce malignancy into children's rapidly dividing cells. In this context, uncontrolled applications of polyhalogenated chemicals and pesticides are the causative factors of staggering incidences of sexual impotence in adult Egyptian males. As documented in wildlife,[15] the uninterrupted routine of the Egyptians to diet on excessively intoxicated daily ingredients and to inhale polluted air has engraved the expected side effects on Egyptian males in terms of testicular dysgenesis and disrupted sertoli cell function, thus precipitating impaired germ cell differentiation yielding (i) reduced semen quality and feminization and (ii) carcinoma in situ. Additionally, the outcome of this endless routine is this: ~20-fold higher proportions of the Egyptian general public with mental insufficiency and physical handicaps compared to those in Canadian incidents. The finale of our detailed scrutiny of 151 medical reports of a location plagued with >12% mental and physical impairment of 5-12y children is staggering indeed. It pointed to in-house accidents, acutely ignoramus medical doctors, chronic and inbred medical negligence of follow-up of cases in terms of early and precise laboratory diagnoses, unskilled laboratory technicians, etc. Medical sloppiness ranged from mishandling of mothers while delivering babies to subjecting infants to excessive anesthesia during minor operations.[3,16] Reviewing the medical reporting of handicapped children pointed to meningococcally induced meningitis as the possible causative factor behind >35% cases of mentally handicapped children. Headache and neck stiffness associated with fever, confusion or altered consciousness, vomiting, and photophobia or phonophobia of the newly born infants, as well as nonspecific symptoms such as irritability and drowsiness including rash, were reported. Regrettably, from the very beginning, both pediatrics and general practitioners failed to notice and to report the symptoms for intensive laboratory diagnoses, prompt medical management, and follow-up. To top it all, social workers fail to report and deal with the high proportion of mental and physical handicap of infants of the habitual first-degree relative/cousin marriages—consanguinity. Traditionally these marriages are aimed at maintaining wealth in between culturally and religiously isolated and low socioeconomic families plagued with illiteracy. It is theorized that the closer the genetic relationship between the parents, the greater the risk of birth defects among their children—autosomal recessive genetic disorders. Therefore, it is deemed essential to avail of genetic and social counseling to Egyptians in general and to farmers in the delta and Upper Egypt in particular. Considering the outcome of genetic defects due to 200 years of communal inbreeding within the Amish congregation,[17] it is a simple mathematical extrapolation to conclude the enormity of mental and physical defects to >3,000 years of first-degree relative/cousin marriages in Egypt. The difference here is the Western Amish recognized their burden and allowed the National *Human Genome Research Institute USA to tackle this issue vis-à-vis the Middle Eastern refusal to entertain advances in medical managements in favor of nomadic traditions: drinking camel's urine.*[17] Within this murky and intricate societal mosaic of intolerance and characterization-induced aggression, consequences of rampant corruptions, ruin of morals, failing medical health, etc., in Egypt, it is rather impossible to quantitatively elaborate on the specific contribution of the environmental and societal factors that are disemboweling the basic fabric of the nation.

In this context, societal dilemma and ramification of male impotence and mental retardation of children require parallel medical and psychological management, which are both absolutely beyond the intellectual and financial capabilities of the current Egyptian society and the dispossessed respectively. The outcome is a further precipitation of marital discordance, the collapse of the family unit concomitantly with males' subliming their fear of female sexuality to surface as pitiless, dogmatic narcissism and radicalization to conveniently taming females to males' absolute obedience. An example of ethics-deficient society that is soaked in backward taboos is the heinous crime of a father, Muhammad Abdel Salam, who, on the account of societal labeling and disgrace, strangled his homosexual son and the heinous murder of George Fathy in Alexandria.[16]

Rubbish dumps scattered within large cities are well-situated sources of pollution; for example, free radicals embodied within the matrix of plastic bags manufactured from a prematurely terminated polymerization process are readily extractable in rubbish-containing organic solvents. These extracts of free radicals may (a) directly penetrate skin of handlers and/or (b) trickle into soil and underground water to saturate various vegetation, basic nutrients, fish's and animals' adipose tissues. As a measure of international protection of the environment, different nations, except for Egypt, report yearly consumption of carbamate insecticides to the concerned UN offices, in 100 kg (viz., table 3 of UN periodical).[18]

Incidence of Malaria

Malaria has been a major disease for thousands of years ever since Hippocrates recognized its prevalence throughout the tropics and subtropics worldwide. Without exception, all patients who tested positive for malaria antibodies in circulation showed positive α-FP in serum. The plausible rationale is, infected mosquitoes introduce uninucleate sporozoites into the human host, which rapidly invade hepatic parenchymal cells, resulting in jaundice and slight decrease in serum's Alb together with elevated liver AST and ALT.[19] This supports our contention of malaria's pathology; that is, sporozoites-induced hepatic inflammation leads to necrosis and regeneration upon regression of the inflammatory response. Typical of hepatic APR, after successful treatment of jaundiced malaria patients, the profile of serum proteins returns to normal within a few weeks, indicative of hemolytic transient impairment rather than permanent damage.[20] Thus, it is safe to assume malaria hepatopathy necessitates the release of acute-phase α-FP to restore normal hepatic function.

Incidence of HBP and Syphilis

Although the serum of a 12y virgin and 3 adult females tested positive for IgG and IgM antibodies to *Treponema pallidum*, the causative agent of syphilis, the subjects remained asymptomatic. Cultured vaginal swabs of these cases did not reveal any indication of a new bacterial strain infection expected to release proteins with determinants similar to those of *T. pallidum*. In this milieu, bejel (spirochete *Treponema pallidum*) and other syphilis-like diseases such as yaws (*T. pertenue*) and pinta (*Treponema carateum*), all free-living and anaerobic bacteria, are closely related. Another related microorganism, *Treponema microdentium*, inhabits the mouth of humans as normal flora. These diseases are not necessarily transmitted through sexual contact, but often by direct contact among individuals living under the filthy environmental conditions of the Middle Eastern milieu. All tested negative for HIV 1+2 and syphilis. One female with positive syphilis-like bacteria in serum had 4 children, 2 males with mental handicap, most likely due to the long lineage of preferred cousin marriages; one healthy 5y female; and the 4th was a 7-month-old daughter, confirmed with a CAT scan to have a ~50% atrophied brain. This 7-month-old baby does not entertain ordinary physical functions; for example, she fails to recognize hunger, pain, cold, heat or saltiness, sugary food, etc. It is safe to assume that the filthy milieu allowed this syphilis-like bacterium and/or others to subsist on the newly formed zygote post in the early hours of fertilization. In this instance, bacteria most likely chewed cells responsible for the buildup of the brain mass, thus inflecting the observed mental incapacitation. It is equally plausible that an infected prostate could precipitate the same side effects. In general, more than 95% of adults and children of this location tested positive for malaria and α-FP in serum. Additionally, >80% stool samples of >5-60y females of this location tested positive for *Enterobius (Oxyuris) vermicularis,* known to possibly infect the fallopian tube, yielding inflammation, tubal obstruction, and infertility.[21]

According to the astounding filth of this location, it is not surprising:

(I)   ~90% of females of this group tested positive for *HBP*,

(II)   Due to chronic colonization of *HBP* of <10y children's gastric mucosa, they weighed 35%-40% less than the average Canadian counterparts do. Albeit incessantly inflamed hepatocytes displayed $10\pm2\%$ depression of biosynthesized total serum proteins relative to healthy Canadian controls, 2D-IEP of this group's plasma revealed a 1.4 ± 0.2-fold increase in the relative concentrations of Fb, Hg, CRP, and AGP. The most unusual case was a 23y female whose ~60-fold increase in plasma Fb regressed to control levels within 120 hours, indicative of acute but transient inflammation,

(III) heat, filth and all year round female head covers facilitated the duplication of a super-bug-head lice resistant to eradication with known lice sprays and kerosene,

(IV) regardless of gender and age, many individuals developed an acute E Coli infestation of the colon and rectum. Most strains of E. Coli bacteria are harmless, however, some are fatally injurious to precipitate kidney failure, haemolytic uremic syndrome and inflammation of the colon. The latter, would most likely initiate the sequence of catabolism of the mucosal layer, and developing rectal polyp associated with bleeding and diarrhoea/constipation. As well, one of the side effects of the culture of exaggerated prescription of antimicrobial drugs is the proliferation of clostridium difficile which is a causative factor of the rampant inflammation of the colon among the disadvantaged of this location. The obvious risk is the transformation of benign colon polyps over time into malignant tumors, and

(V) A significant 17% of females aged 19-45y were diagnosed to harbour Toxoplasma gondii. Pregnant females embracing this insult could pass it to their embryos with the concomitant risks of developing major disorders of nervous system, mental retardation, eye and heart damage.

The perception is that gastritis is a symptom of proliferating *HBP* into gastric mucosa, thus provoking inflammation and the biosynthesis of specific APR proteins. *HBP*-induced APR, together with preexisting high blood pressure and elevated concentrations of cholesterol and long-chain-saturated triacylglycerols in serum, may be a contributing factor[22] to the high proportion of children's early death by myocardial infarction in these ghettos. It could be contemplated that incubation of *HBP* into animals' gastric mucosa, provoking myocardial infarction and eventual death, is a necessity within the natural mechanism of events in the cycle of life to provide the earth with necessary nutrients for plantation. This is a microscale distant event where during the course of evolution, large animals such as dinosaurs were the prey to much smaller ones. Currently, the integrity of the bionetwork may necessitate mammalian casualty by bacterial infection. Nonetheless, it is equally plausible; *HBP* may not be the sole factor inducing hepatic APR in patients with cardiac maladies. Psychological stress resulting from isolation and fear emanating from societal rejection[23,24] could also be among the very many factors contributing to the observed elevation of APR proteins. Accordingly, APR proteins released in response to *HBP* incubation of gastric mucosa may not be the major causative factor behind, or the rate-limiting step to, cardiac maladies but, rather, a postevent APR of hepatocytes to cardiac injuries. In conclusion, homeless Egyptians dwelling in these staggeringly filthy ghettos became the culture media for a wide range of viral/bacterial insults to breed. Thus, it is alluring to assume that long-term infectious contact would, most likely, induce bacterial/ viral mutations as well as potentiate adaptive viral/bacterial lateral gene transfer into hosts' DNA; that is, intramolecular reorganization of the recipient's gene is a viable conclusion. Should Horizontal transfer of bacterial/viral regenerative genetic material into hosts' DNA materialize, it is likely to induce exponential regenerative activity in recipient's site of mutated DNA, e.g., a malignant tumor. This theoretical scheme of events, together with environmental intoxication, may rationalize the recently observed high proportions of 3rd-generation homeless children developing a broad span of malignancies.

Autoimmune Rejection of End-Stage Cirrhotic Liver Together with Other Organs

Clinical data and autoimmune-induced rejection of the liver in an animal model support the thesis of immune rejection of cirrhotic liver and possibly other organs, leading to the expiry of patients. 2D-IEP of intraperitoneally (IP) aspirated exudates from late-stage HCV patients (a) showed a mirror-image spectrum of plasma proteins to those of serum proteins and (b) embraced CHO, TG, Glu, urea, UA acid, AST, and ALT. This phenomenon suggests acute inflammation-induced increased porosity of the circulatory system, leading to filtration of serum proteins and other factors into the peritoneum. Nonetheless, positive testing of AST and ALT in the peritoneal exudates could possibly be accounted for by assuming the disintegration of the hepatic tissue, emancipating its cellular contents, including ML enzymes, in the peritoneal cavity. Hepatic ML hydrolases would degrade hepatic and other organs' tissue. Thus, biosynthesis and release of antibodies to disintegrated hepatic and other organs' tissues are an inevitability that ultimately leads to multi-immune rejection of the liver together with other organs, that is, the hastened expiry of patients.

We found it indispensable to develop an animal model to verify the hypothesized biomechanics of liver rejection as a possible causative factor promoting the expiry of end-stage HCV patients. Healthy male rabbits were subcutaneously inoculated with rabbit-liver homogenate in Freund's adjuvant; within the first 2 weeks post inoculation, 4 rabbits showed signs of accumulation of peritoneal exudation. Two-dimensional-IEP and chemistry of collected PF showed the same protein pattern, together with parallel proportions of CHO, Glu, TG, urea, UA, AST, and ALT to those of the rabbit's serum. Comparable concentration of circulatory serum proteins were found in the urine and CSF of inflamed rabbits (table 4). Although PC-model calculation of charge distribution on and molecular volume of cholesterol, glucose, triacylglycerols, urea, and uric acid molecules differed substantially, the efficiency of the release of the said factors in ascetic fluid was similar. This is a further confirmation of the release of these components into animals' peritoneal cavity via the disintegration of inflamed hepatocytes *vis-à-vis* inflammatory mediators or enzyme-assisted filtration into peritoneum. Histological examination of hepatic tissue indicated apoptosis, macrovascular fatty changes, and massive hepatic necrosis. Furthermore, concomitant discharge of hepatic lytic ML-hydrolases into the rabbits' peritoneum is expected to subject the liver and other organs to massive disintegration. Thus, autodegradation and apoptosis of end-stage HCV hepatic tissue would turn the peritoneal cavity into a reservoir accommodating the refuse and debris of bursting organs and their various metabolites. This eventually leads to the biosynthesis of antibodies to hepatic and other tissues, thus baptizing organ rejection. Therefore, immune rejection of cirrhotic liver mass and, possibly, other organs is an acceptable postulate to the finale of end-stage HCV patients. At this stage, obviously, the close to or below healthy levels of ALT and AST in the serum and the PF of end-stage HCV patients do not necessarily imply healing; rather, they are indicative of the substantially low mass of bursting viable hepatic tissue, and/or the metabolically fatigued liver is biosynthesizing inactive ALT and AST precursors; that is, the enzymatic-core protein is void of specific molecular arrangement characteristics of corresponding enzymatic activity. Therefore, it is most beneficial to medically manage HCV patients with or without renal failure prior to the exudation of body fluids into the peritoneal cavity to (a) evade problems emancipated with the perpetual drainage of the exudate fluids of patients and (b) impede, if possible, immune rejection of liver mass and other organs leading to their expiry (viz., scheme 1).

As mentioned above, a controlled diet enriched with natural supplements has modestly decreased the metabolic load on fatigued hepatocytes; that is, it allows partial restoration of the hepatic faculty pertaining to the biosynthesis and export of plasma proteins into circulation. Furthermore, a natural diet together with periodical removal of HCV-4b patients' serum with equal volume of synthetic analog would definitely improve health conditions of the Egyptian dispossessed stricken with chronic hepatic maladies and concomitantly burdened crushing poverty, unable to afford daily bread. To expand on this possibility, our preliminary trials were carried out on a 1 kg healthy rabbit model. Daily withdrawal of 10 mL blood at 8:00 a.m. and separating plasma and resuspending blood cells in a 6 mL solution of our preparation of organic/inorganic constituents similar to L-15 media were carried out under aseptic conditions. This blood-cell suspension in a 10 mL synthetic solution was intravenously (IV) introduced 30 minutes later into the same rabbit. During experiments, drinking water was supplemented with the same prepared organic/

inorganic mixture. 2D-IEP of experimental rabbits' serum on the 10th day embraced 85%-93% of serum proteins. Moreover, visual microscopic examination of a histological preparation of experimental hepatic tissue documented no lesions on hepatic cellular constituents; also, concentrations of hepatic intracellular acid-hydrolases were not elevated, indicative of stress-free mechanisms of biosynthesis of serum proteins without major degradation to hepatic intracellular structure. Further experimentations are necessary to inquire into industrial preparations of synthetic plasma and the viability of displacing plasma in end-stage HCV-4b patients with synthetic plasma-fluid enriched with the minimal range of monomeric amino acids, carbohydrates, and low-molecular-weight unsaturated fatty acids necessary for the hepatic intracellular machinery to biosynthesize plasma and intracellular proteins.

The Social Element

Over and above HBV, HCV, *HBP*, and other pathogens plaguing the destitute Egyptians, all indications are characterizing a resigned population heavily burdened by deeply rooted scars of psychological abuse and afflictions. The pointer is the >3:1 ratio of females to males in the <10y group, which could be rationalized in terms of the heavily polluted environment and psychological load yielding frail and low counts of male sperms. The immediate impact of this phenomenon is already fermenting social havoc emanating from two abundant and contradictory mass media pursuits: (a) narcissistic male sermons advocating the inferiority of and the anointing of women as the absolute subject to men's whim, and (b) copious pornography on free satellite channels. Our observations are supported by recent reports suggesting poverty and the decline of morals and values, among other factors, as causative to the increase in rates of violence against women.[25] Over 500 cases of sexual harassment, 19 murders of women, 8 cases of rape, frighteningly high rates of kidnappings, and suicides of females were emphasized in terms of psychological violence that is no less severe than physical violence. For example, in Alexandria, a leading gynecologist had to deal with a case of a traumatized 3y female raped by an elderly 35-year-old, the first cousin of the mother; a homeless person picked and married a 10y female (*Al-Masry Al-Youm*, September 29, **2006**); a kidnapped 4y female child was sexually assaulted by the janitor (*Al-Masry Al-Youm*, June 11, **2007**); a gang of 4 sexually assaulted 1 female and 7 male homeless children (*Al Messa*, April 6, **2007**); Ibrahim Salama Hamad, Ibrahim Muslim Ayad, Hatem Mahmoud, and Muhammad Salama were charged of beating Youssef and mating with his fiancée (*Al Messa*, March 1, **2007**); Muhammad Mustafa el Sayied attains his satisfaction masturbating after touching and injuring his female victims with a sharp blade (*Al Gomhuria*, March 1, **2009**), in the city Port Said, two sisters 23y Hana'a and 16y Asma'a of Radwan village reported (**case 2497/2012**) they were coerced to sexual intercourse with their 48y father Salamah for a period of one and three months respectively, Ramadan of the village of Showni/Tanta accused his brother Muhamad of mating his daughter Ha'eyam (**case 63** Tanta), certain brother Ahmed killed his sister for copulating with her cousin, etc. Although reported figures are high, the actual numbers are greater, as many cases go unreported in the country. Most recently, George Fathy was murdered and his corpse was mutilated. Many assumed the killing of George to be a conspicuous manifestation of the sectarian feud in Alexandria. Most likely, events of this heinous murder point to street justice executed by dogmatically oblivious characters, especially two years earlier, one of them was murdered for the same reason. There were many early indications to George's homosexuality; however, psychological managements of his aberrations were frustrated according to dogmatic reasoning, and he was evaded as a leper. Unfortunately, his last random attempt at persuading masculine individuals for sexual favors was denied, and it turned ugly; he was murdered. In a society whose conscience is raped by fundamentalism, the ignoramus populace, failing to comprehend the possibility of genetic aberrations settling humans' description of sexual orientation, would opt to atrocious justice to settle genetically impelled different behavior. Similarly, as discussed in this presentation, pollution-induced infertility may conceive specificity of sexual preferences, and other causative factors such as differences in the brains of homosexuals, hormonal differences, and early familial or intra-abuse of children may account for behavioral and sexual trends. However, leading theologians unaware of above said factors plausibly precipitating given sexual orientations decided this: gay marriage was one of the several threats to the traditional family and undermines "the future of humanity itself." Thus, consequences of the threat to civilization (e.g., pollution, societal injustice, bifurcation of a population of the same and one nation according to religious orientation, low-grade education plagued with dogmatic militancy, rampant ignorance, and failure of secular institutions) were dwarfed into the righteous preferences of hormonal activity. According to our observations, in the absence of female experimental animals, mature male rats or rabbits are inclined to mate with weaker males especially when crowded (e.g., 9-12 male individuals per animal cage).

The acute pollution of the environment (e.g., air, potable water, basic food ingredients, etc.) would most likely precipitate low counts of male sperms, which may account for the >3 ratio of female/male of <10y group, that is, imbalanced reproduction of the two genders *vis-à-vis* the statistically accepted distribution in healthy societies. The immediate social impact of this radically crooked proportion, together with a lack of sex education, has increased inadequate intimacy. This is expected to ferment social ills, crimes, and organic diseases; that is, probabilities of shuttling new subtypes of venereal diseases to environments at a close transportation distance are increased. It is our contention that collective measures of societal dogmatic neurosis have impelled the disadvantaged of *ul-Makkaber* to establish psychological and other protective barriers to maintain their milieu intact and resistant to outside interference. Deprivation of the destitute of their natural rights, medical attention, and education would turn their enclaves into fertile crucibles, subliming societal labeling and poverty into mental neurosis, yielding desperate acts of (i) dogmatic intolerance and female mutilations to mainly cover intellectual and organic male impotency, thus reflecting a typical fear of minorities and female sexuality respectively, and (ii) resenting the unavailable medical management, which coerces illiterates to entertain notorious recipes of drinking camel's urine as a natural substitute to medicate malignancy, HCV, hair loss, etc. Camel urine products are going viral in Egypt as shampoo, cosmetics, as well it is available in capsules and as oil of camel's urine. According to newspapers' advertisements, expensive camel urine is abundantly available in well-established camel farms near Alexandria and other spots by the Mediterranean shore.

Although occupants of some of these enclaves are masqueraded in devoutness, the prevailing psychological aberrations, together with illiteracy-induced low self-esteem, have contributed to sporadic cases of incest. Rather than having social workers and psychiatrists tackle this particular dilemma to unravel its core, (i.e., the burden of the social fabric propelled incest offenders to cheat), they opted for denial and dogmatic interpretations of pious elders. Under filthy and life-threatening conditions, young females are obliged to terminate their pregnancies by unskilled midwives. A 24y male slaughtered his brother for having sex with their sisters and their mother (*Al-Masry Al-Youm,* June 14, **2008**). In a similar situation of societal volatility and communal decline and in desperation to attain an innate spiritual quest, ancient ancestors cynically manipulated their gods. A 4,000y Theban script described impoverished Egyptians cheating their gods (e.g., offering them a sacrifice of geese in lieu of well-fed oxen).

As of the 1952 coup, poverty and mental bankruptcy hatched very many fat cats with ruined morals to precipitate the following phenomenon:

(a) Some individuals, heavily burdened by poverty, are driven into unhygienic routes to achieve facile richness. For example, catfish cultured in germ-infested sewage, feeding on manure polluted with a wide spectrum of environmental toxins until it weighs ~12 kg are minced to feed cultured shrimp. Thus, mad-shrimp disease à la mad cow disease is expected to flourish among tourists, the very few who can afford expensive shrimp meals at expensive restaurants and luxurious hotels. On the other hand, detailed GLC of muscle and abdominal triacylglycerols of catfish collected from Mahmoudiyah Canal in Alexandria documented the spectrum of saturated long-chain triacylglycerols characteristic to mammals. This may be (a) the outcome of catfish feeding on abundantly roaming rats or corpses of animals thrown in the Mahmoudiyah Canal and/or (b) a marker of the possible evolution of catfish into amphibian species; that is, the first tetrapods evolved from their aquatic ancestors, undergoing many structural and functional mutations where limbs developed from lobe fins, presumably to allow terrestrial locomotion. That is, fish evolved into *amphibia, amphibians* into primates, and primates into man.

(b) Because of the dogma-induced mental trauma, Egyptian laypersons are unable to recognize the threat of an imminent HCV-4b genocide harvesting their lives. According to available medical reports, treatment of HCV-4b patients with a combination of pegylated interferon α-2b and ribavirin is associated with low response rates and high incidence of side effects. According to medical ethics, clinical, biochemical, and histological inquiry to detect responders to pegylated interferon α-2b and ribavirin treatment should precede medical prescriptions. This is an essential issue as the pegylated interferon α-2b and ribavirin treatment is physically and economically demanding. In state and private hospitals, HCV patients are abused by the greed-driven MDs. It is well documented that 80% of HCV-positive Egyptians are in contact with subtype 4b; however, the price-inflated interferon and ribavirin are uselessly administered on weekly bases to elderly patients with late-stage HCV liver cirrhosis for more than a year, without prior diagnostic confirmation of the efficacy of the treatment. To salvage the ~20% of Egyptians with HCV-1, local MDs have to realize that in HCV-1 patients, very promising results have been reported when the protease inhibitor telaprevir or boceprevir is added to the medical recipe. It increases the sustained virological response rates from ~50% on pegylated interferon plus ribavirin to

70%, managed by a combination of pegylated interferon, ribavirin plus telaprevir. Diagnostic assays of serum of most Egyptian HCV-4b patients managed for a year with interferon and ribavirin documented deterioration of hepatic function. Most illogical, administrations of the very same privately owned hospitals, whose specialists failed to manage HCV-4b patients with staggering rates of death, whose pediatrics failed to report cases of newborns with meningitis, etc., are entertaining liver transplants to surgically manage HCV cirrhosis. Assuming the availability of a well-trained team of microsurgeons, qualified nurses, acceptable sanitary intensive care milieu, etc., the net result is that entertaining this option is ridiculous. It could be anticipated with certainty that 25% of the Egyptian populace would develop end-stage HCV cirrhosis; if surgical liver transplant is entertained as an option, would it imply excision of healthy livers of 25% of the population? Most likely, if this venture would materialize, it is tailored to suit the welfare of the few oil-wealthy individuals with cirrhotic livers on sex tours of Egypt (*Ad-Dustour,* June 15, **2008**). At best, healthy livers would be purchased from the dispossessed with less than $1,000-2,000 or involuntarily harvested (*Ad-Dustour,* May 13, **2008**). An example of the very many is best illustrated in http://ipsnews.net/news.asp?idnews=47738:

> CAIRO, Jul 21, 2009 (IPS)-Karim borrowed money to expand his bakery. When the money ran out and the business became sour, he failed to pay his debts; accordingly he faced the prospect of imprisonment. The only option left for the 36-year-old Egyptian baker is to sell his kidney. According to same reporting, the absence of legislation regulating human organ transplants has made Egypt an international "hotspot" for kidney trafficking. Up to 95 percent of the 3,000 legal kidney transplants per year, and hundreds of illegal ones, involve a commercial transaction.

A kidney can be purchased for as low as US$15,000 on Cairo's black market; the donor only receives about $2,500, and the rest goes to hospitals, laboratories, and agents. A Washington-based NGO, Coalition for Organ-Failure Solutions (COFS), working to end organ trafficking, reveals an alarming trend: poverty is driving Egyptians to sell their organs. In general, the donors are misled about the risks and talked into taking examinations at hospitals and private labs. The results are used to match donors to clients, often wealthy Gulf Arabs, who use forged documents to circumvent a ban on transplants to unrelated or non-Egyptian recipients. In a dogmatically plagued nation, the clerics added their motifs to deprive the populace of these sophisticated medical advances; for example, organ transplants are considered a trespass against the Creator, as human organs are a gift from Him to humans but remain His property. Thus, under no circumstance do humans have dominance over their organs, including donation for transplantation into a needy recipient. Furthermore, organ transplant is a forbidden medical procedure as it wrecks the prearranged expiry of the diseased to meet with the Creator[17] just as artificial insemination of a female married to an impotent male is fornication and a sin.[17] Most recently, the head of the Egyptian medical union restricted organ transplant to a dogmatically compatible donor and recipient (www.masrawy.com/News/Egypt/Politics/**2008**/august/17/organs.aspx*).* Recently, many at the bottom scale of intelligence suggested razing the sphinx and pyramids. These taboos would turn organ donation into a lucrative behind-the-scene donor trafficking where brokers lurk in the coffee shops of Cairo slums, targeting the poor. The recent 2012 ghoulish train accidents in Egypt documented beyond a shed of doubt the utter failure and indifference to rescue the victims, viz., *two trains collide in Badrashin,* (***July 2012, injuring 44***)*, train crashes into several cars in Qalyub, Qalubiya governorate* (***October 2012, killing six and injuring dozens***)*, two trains collide near Fayoum in Upper Egypt* (***November 2012, killing three people, including the driver, and injuring 46***) *and another crashes into a bus carrying schoolchildren on a railway crossing in Manfalout village, Assiut governorate.* (***November 2012, Kills 51, mostly children, injures 17***). The filth of operation rooms and emergency wards, lack of minimal required items as antibiotics, syringes, sanitized gauze together with the ethical bankruptcy of the theocratic state of Mursi to compassionately address disasters claiming the very many lives of dispossessed Egyptians became the norm of day life in Egypt. Most recently, in two private hospitals, the authors caught laboratory technicians tailoring results of serum's chemistry. In brief, it is tiresome to entertain the transplantation of liver portions as it would pose a threat to the lives of both the recipient and the donor. The obvious and most acceptable alternative is the noninvasive liver-dialysis technique or periodical infusion with synthetic analogs replacing the same volume of already circulating plasma. However, considering the notorious and failing sanitary standards of Egyptian hospitals, the option of liver dialysis should be pondered with extreme circumspection. Utter filth and failing of sanitary standards within Egyptian kidney dialysis wards in private hospitals promote infection with mutant bacterial and viral diseases resistant to medical management with known medications.

(c) In early 2009, and in fear of H1N1, the population went into a brutal dogmatic passion of killing hogs. This peculiar behavior may be rationalized according to the conceptualization of *the God gene.* That is, genes are hardwiring the pious inclinations of humans, accordingly setting the modality of daily life. Thus, the manifestation of the God gene and its reorganization into sects according to the cultural milieu of a tribe is the yield of several factors: neurobiological, psychological, behavioral, genetic, and environmental ones. It is our contention that the environmental factor limited to the abundance or aridness of natural resources has principally tailored the heritable God gene VMAT2, whose configuration is bound to specific monoamine levels. Extrapolation of the same chain of organic evolutionary thoughts to the God gene yields interesting theologies pertaining to the evolution and devolution of monotheism.

In conclusion, (a) The conceptualization of a "just society" is chronically peculiar at both national and local levels, especially the current theocratic establishment, which is either yielding to or liaising with dogmatic οχλοκρατία (mobocracy); thus, measures to reverse this trend are not to be expected in the immediate or the very near future, if at all. Therefore, an multidisciplinary international preventive scheme utilizing a biomedical, psychological, and educational approach is deemed essential to resolve the current HCV genocide at its source and to salvage the cradle of civilization, Egypt. This option will not only ease the plight of dispossessed Egyptians but will also avert the possibility of exporting mutated viral and bacterial diseases to Europe and to North America. (b) As much as Ugandan children developed Kaposi's sarcoma at the late stages of HIV, it is worthwhile to monitor HCV-4b Egyptian homeless for developing specific tumors and HCV *de novo* mutants. (c) The axis of dire medical care of a society whose fabric is soaked with radical dogmatism and is void of righteous consciousness, democracy, and liberalism while coercing its intellectual pillars into silence by the theocratic remnants of the corrupt dictatorship of the 1952 junta colonels has already set the genocide tunes for Egypt, a 7,000-year-old nation. By all means, the prospects of not only the destitute Egyptians, but of all the Egyptians, are bleak if they have any.

In the final analysis: The pertinent question is pertaining to the wisdom of applying top-of-the-art scientific dialectics to societies whose occupants are disemboweled of reason and ready to lynch whoever utters a rationally sound critique of the sayings of their ancestors. The portrayal below is self-explanatory and sums it all up: tribal richness, oil dollars invested in a twisted, rusty rocket and wondering goats.

It is safe to theorize that supporting specific individuals for life to ensure the flow of crude oil would aggravate poverty and cause the erosion of the middle and the working classes; also, favoring consumerism would ultimately lead to corrupt, low standards of life and increased medical risks and pathogens' mutations to *de novo* genotypes. With facile transportation, abundant demand for cheap labor in Germany and France, and the attraction of London life for the dons of oil, these *de novo* mutants are easily exported into Europe and North America. This is supported by the reported statistical incidence of HCV in Germany, UK, France, and Italy in comparison to Monaco, Sweden, and Denmark that points to immigrant workers from the Middle East and Africa as the causative factor (http://www.rightdiagnosis.com/h/hepatitis_c/stats-country.htm#extrapwarning). That is, financial gains made by the multinationals are temporary and short-lived as they are counterbalanced by exposing the health of laymen/women to risks of contracting mutants resistant to known medications. In response, pharmaceuticals will provide consumers with speedily tested medications without an in-depth search into its side effects; for example, antidepressant intake during pregnancy may raise risk of autism in newly born infants. Apoptosis of the human race? In general, HCV is associated with a lower quality of life and increased loss of work productivity, and depletion of health care resources among the adult EU population. Our conclusions parallel previous studies conducted using the US and Japan NHWS databases (*http://www.natap.org/2011/EASL/EASL_110.htm*). *In this context, it is perplexing indeed to have the media attention drawn to side effects of first-and secondhand smoking while ignoring the dilemma of spelling and refining crude oil and the firsthand inhaling of air permanently polluted by car and industrial exhaust. Our preliminary data* on rat models that were fed chew pellets enriched with 3% condensate of destructive decomposition of fuel *documented (i) induction of APR without regression leading to irreversible* liver cirrhosis and that (ii) implants of Yoshida sarcoma (YS) grew in weight 60% faster in said intoxicated animals, thus hastening expiry of host rats as well; recurrence of YS tumor postsurgical removal of the original 5-d tumor was 2-fold faster in rats that were fed polluted diets *versus* YS controls.

The computer doctor: Above is a vivid elaboration on the ramification of corrupt societal principles impregnated with educational failure, academically bankrupt MDs, inefficient but expensive medical care in filthy hospitals, abundance of barber doctors performing surgical mutilation of females and prescribing camel's urine as a pious ancestral recipe to cure HCV and various carcinogenic tumors, poor communication with the technical revolution and advanced methodologies in medicine, radical poverty of laypersons, etc. Thus, peaceful intervention of Western medical might is inevitable. We are advocating the "computer doctor." Together with well-known Canadian MDs specializing in handling a wide spectrum of toxin-induced male impotency, hepatic diseases, tropical bacterial and viral insults, etc., we are initiating the concept of computer doctors. That is, data of diagnoses pertaining to body fluids of the unfortunate population will be fed into computers with special software to itemize the geneses and parameters of maladies according to the tailored database. Furthermore, it is more realistic if scientists from their corners of comfort in basic research would visualize the toil of Bill Gates to eradicate diseases in India. This is to tackle the geneses of the many toxicological and medical threats plaguing the underdeveloped world before it is too late.

Bill Gates is trying to eliminate polio. The number of children paralyzed by the polio virus was reduced from 350,000 in 1998 to fewer than 225 cases in 2012. However, pockets of the debilitating disease in Afghanistan, Nigeria and Pakistan, must be cleared or else it will make a comeback. Nonetheless, in absolute agreement with our conclusion, the very same radical melancholia μελαγχολία of conspiracy theories are trying to frustrate his efforts. The chain reaction which initiated this macabre trend was triggered in 1916; T. E. Lawrence effectively managed the Arab irregular troops, under the command of Emir Faisal bin Hussein, in protracted guerrilla operations to dismantle the Ottoman Empire with minimal damage to Britain, if there was any. In 2010, it is safe to assume Obama's tailoring of the so-called Arab Spring was to primarily impede the mushrooming of the Chinese economy and eviscerate any possibilities of Russian resurrection. Considering the ease of communications and facile transfer of knowledge and intra—and intercontinental shuttling, Obama's Arab Spring is anticipated to usher the collapse of new Rome specifically baptized by the dubious event of the murder of the USA ambassador to a new member of the states of Arab Spring, Libya. In Old Rome, the assassination of Gnaeus Pompeius Magnus (Pompey) dissipated the dreams of a parliamentary republic. Pompey, a product of wealthy Italian nobility, at a very young 35y of age advanced to first council of Rome and meteorically rose to power. Alas, he was decapitated while heading for what appeared to be a welcoming party on the shores of Alexandria/Egypt. It became a habit; Gaius Julius Caesar, an ex-ally and a father-in-law of Pompey, was assassinated in the Roman senate. As of that time, Rome was ruled by whoever could lavishly bribe army gladiators, military-multinational complex? In today's Rome, the assassination of Robert Kennedy deracinated the utopian dreams of a just society.

The equation is very simple and obvious. It is the choice between maintaining the fabric of the Western working class as viable as possible in terms of providing education and medical care at minimal costs possible at private or public educational and health institutions respectively. This is to maximize the extraction of wealth from nature as in the scientific advances of first human landing on the moon, medical innovations to manage acute diseases, *versus* the induced political havoc of the so-called Arab's spring. Although it was tailored to secure the importation of crude oil for the sake of lucrative accrual of wealth for the very few, ultimately it would lead to the chronic recession of the mental faculties together with deterioration in educational standards and health care of the natives. The fatal far reaching consequences are the importation of second generation mutated bacterial and viral diseases from these volatile Arab spring states? For example, the 'Saudi SARS' is the tentative name of a newly discovered *coronavirus*. Early reports compared the virus to SARS. The virus first emerged in the Middle East, and was discovered on September 2012 in a Qatari man from Saudi Arabia. He was treated for respiratory disease and renal failure. The first Saudi Arabian to contract the disease died early 2012. Closer scrutiny reveals some multinationals have released questionable food additives as sucrose polyester, aspartame, genetically modified food, etc., into North American and European food markets. In this context, (i) professional consideration of the research data carried out by Procter & Gamble, to support FDA approval of sucrose polyester as a food additive, embodies contradictions to its safety for human consumption, (ii) many sites are available to the addictive carcinogenic-neurotoxicity of aspartame, and (iii) we recently found extracted peel oil of Tangerine Sequoia # 4383 Minneola is capable of extracting chemicals of plastic utensils available at Price Chopper, Yankee One Dollar and Dollar tree stores.

Thus, it could be concluded with certainty, at this precarious point of time, the seeds of global disasters are exponentially germinating. Thus, the few brave toxicologists warring against global warming, depletion of ozone layer, intoxication of nature and wild life, etc., could appreciate the agonizing tribulations which haunted the crying pure soul in the wilderness, John the Baptist, before his decapitation. Accordingly, we are allowed to momentarily depart from the scientific context to delve into the conceptualization: should the toxicologists of today have the courage and steadfastness of John the Baptist, implementation of rules to curb intoxication and to ease the burden of the human misery of the disadvantaged should be feasible.

Societal Characterization Induced Hepatic Acute Phase Response An Animal Model

A rat animal model was developed to mimic the exposure of the dispossessed in Egypt to the injurious stress emanating from societal labeling and characterization. In the model, rats were exposed to different arrangements of psychological stress, a combination of different schedules of feeding and recorded sounds of cats in fierce fighting. Unscheduled stress and irregular feeding evoked an APR indicative of neurobiological activation of a physiological chain of events leading to gastritis and hepatic insults. Present data suggest erratic and long-term psychological abrasions would precipitate various physiological injuries, thus inducing hepatic APR en route to evoking cardiac maladies. Nonetheless, acclimatization of the experimental animal model to the psychophysiological stimulus for longer periods of time, 7-15d documented regression of APR. This is indicative of possible defensive biological internalization of psychological traumata, but not necessarily healing.

Although model animals were raised and kept aseptically, a psychological-provocation-induced injury revealed different onset and regression of APR spectra according to the arrangement of the applied stimulant. Therefore, it is safe to assume that the neurological or psychological decoding of a rat's perception and its reaction to external aggression threatening its physical existence is *engraved* within its DNA mapping. This psychological DNA mapping is quantitatively inherited and is expected to be expressed at an opportune circumstance, regardless of conditions of animal's breeding.

Introduction

The ultimate urge of the presentation is to elaborate on the organic damaging effects of the psychological loading of individuals from the stress of authoritarian societal labeling, targeting their specificities such as dogmatic inclinations, gender, societal status, etc. Thus, multiplicities of convoluted emotions are evoked within the psyche of the two parties, the antagonists and the humbled. Intricacies and anatomy of this neurotic obsession with piety *à la The Promotion of Virtue and Prevention of Vice* that is rampant in Middle Eastern culture is deemed essential for the preservation of our species *vis-à-vis* the futilities of wars. Furthermore, results of our initial experimentations point to the possibilities of APR serum markers to screen individuals with specific instinctive belligerences. Destitute occupants of the two major ghettos, *ul-Makkaber a*nd *ul-Zabbaleen*, and other sporadic enclaves, besides living far below the medically accepted norms, are (i) embedded in excessively polluted milieu and (ii) societally characterized and labeled. Regardless of education, Egyptians are alert to immediate gossip and instantaneous categorization of others according to socioeconomic distinctions, race, gender, and dogmatic affiliation and (iii) deprived of their rights to decent varieties of nourishment, refined education, etc., thus being intentionally kept in a quagmire of backwardness. This combination of medical and social elements may be the ultimate factor contributing to the observation that ~12% of infants are born with mental retardation and contracting cancerous tumors at a tender age and ~15% of 15-20y are addicted to narcotics, etc.

Initially, electrical stimulation of the amygdala produces sustained attention and orienting reactions. If the stimulation continues, fear and/or rage reactions are elicited. Amygdaloid stimulation can also result in intense changes in facial expression. These include facial contortions, baring of the teeth, dilation of the pupils, widening or narrowing of the eyelids, flaring of the nostrils, tearing, as well as sniffing, licking, and chewing. In many instances, stimulation of the amygdala results in anger, irritation, and rage, which seem to gradually build up until finally, the animal/human will attack. Thus, amygdaloid activation results in attacks directed at something real. Moreover, ramifications of rage and aggression may endure and linger well beyond the termination of the electrical stimulation of the amygdala. In fact, the amygdala remains electrophysiologically active post-termination of the stimulus. On the other hand, within minorities, perception of psychological overloads of societal rejections and sentiments of dogmatic characterization by the amygdala would activate the alarm system, that is, the hypothalamic-pituitary-adrenal axis (HPA) and the sympathetic nervous system. While the HPA is a complex set of interactions among the hypothalamus, the pituitary gland, and the adrenal glands, the sympathetic nervous system readies the individual to mobilize the body's resources under *stress* to induce the *fight-or-flight* response. HPA is a major part of the *neuroendocrine system* that controls reactions to stress and regulates many body processes (e.g., *digestion*, the *immune system*, emotions, sexuality, and energy storage and expenditure). Activation of HPA is expected to yield pathologically inflamed livers to a wide array of injuries. In this perspective, ~12% of the passive population of *ul-Zabbaleen's* ghetto is predominantly diabetic and in long-term contact with atherosclerosis and autoimmune diseases,[23] culminating in death at young age. By contrast, in the more aggressive milieu of *ul-Makkaber*, while occupants are physically drained into addiction to narcotics and satellite pornography, it is intentionally arranged to efficiently consume the limited mental resources of the illiterate masses into daily and weekly dogmatically charged TV sermons, in which listeners are bombarded with dogmatic militarism of behavioral dictates, slogans, etc. (viz., pertinent literature).[24] Nonetheless, psychological aberrations, together with poverty-ignited crimes, are fueled by dogmatic intolerance. Recent reports[25, 26] that explored the connection between the nervous system and the inflammatory response to disease support the current hypothesis of psychological stress inducing hepatic APR, thus precipitating a wide array of organic injuries. It is also feasible that culminating organic bodily injuries due to stress would provoke hepatic APR.

In general, 2D-IEP of serum of Egyptian laypersons showed a depressed pattern of identified proteins in the serum of tested individuals relative to healthy Canadian controls. This is most likely a spectrum of APR pertaining to the decoding of multi-inflammatory stimuli emanating from subjecting the Egyptians to concomitant organic and psychological insults. For accurate quantitation of the hepatic APR to psychological aggravation and characterization, we were prompted to examine a rat model under defined experimental conditions, that is, to briefly inquire into the induction of APR to synthesized psychological stress.

Two distinctive sets of psychological injuries were developed:

(a) ***Unscheduled Psychological Stress in Animal Model:*** At random intervals, 6-9 times per day, rats were irregularly offered chew and water for 10 minutes for the duration of 10-30 minutes each, with the recorded sound of cats in fierce fighting either prior to, post, or during availability of chew and water. In a second set, rats were exposed to similar treatment but during the darkness of the night.

(b) ***Scheduled Psychological Stress:*** Rats were freely offered chew and water in the early morning (8:00 a.m.) and late afternoon (6:00 p.m.) while playing the same recorded sound of fighting cats for 20 minutes.

Discussion

Neurosis-Induced APR: In the current experimental model, daylight exposure of rats to *unscheduled* psychological stress evoked an orthodox APR spectrum in terms of (i) increased relative concentrations of AGP, Hg, and Fb and (ii) decreased relative concentrations of Alb and pre-Alb, which lasted for the duration of the experiment, 15 days (table 5a). Regression of APR as of the 7th day does not necessarily imply healing, but most likely a muted APR phenomenon to extra organic injuries precipitated by the psychological load. The steady increase in serum glucose, 1.2 ± 0.03-fold on day 15, may suggest either pancreatic injury and/or substantial catabolism of hepatic intracellular and skeletal proteins and glycoproteins to corresponding organic monomers to provide the hepatic intracellular pool with free amino acids and glucose to biosynthesize defensive APR proteins. In general, repeated episodes of psychologically induced low-grade inflammation in rats, thus activating the innate immune system, would provoke type 2 diabetes, atherosclerosis, etc.[24] By comparison, *unscheduled* psychological stimulation of rat models in the dark hours of the night was found to initiate a higher percentage of APR and faster regression *vis-à-vis* same psychological injury during the day (table 5b). This is suggestive of the ability of the host animal's autoimmune defense to adapt to and internalize *unscheduled* repeated neuro-inflammations in the absence of visual manifestation of the psychological impetus. The phenomenon of internalization of repeated psychological rage was further confirmed, as APR to *scheduled* psychological stress regressed as of day 7 of the experiment, that is, minimization of associated organic injuries, allowing full expression of APR to neuroprovocation *à la* a simple pattern of organic injury (table 6). Furthermore, this observation reflects the ability of the rat model to adapt to an expected and timely *scheduled* psychological signal, especially in the absence of cognitive appraisals of 3-dimensional dramatizations of the psychological thrust. Alternatively, the observed diluted APR could be theorized in terms of hepatocytes response to multi-inflammatory stimulants triggered by experimental psychosis. Thus, rather than regression of APR indicative of healing, it is rather the catabolism of serum proteins/glycoproteins is inevitable to provide hepatic compartments with minimally required carbohydrate and amino acids monomers for survival. In this context, experimental rats do not physically see cats; however, listening to the sound of cats in fierce fighting has precipitated the consequences of their presence in the rat's psyche. This also demonstrates the ability of the biological order to regain equilibrium post initial organic and/or psychological injury. Thus, the animal's recognition of periodic stressful signals may activate a parallel DNA-stored biological defense to obstruct and to internalize the anticipated perpetual stimuli in order to get APR proteins to healthy aseptic levels and to minimize energy expenditure, that is, to maintain the lowest negative entropy of activation possible. This APR could be interpreted as the biological outcome of an early warning mechanism optimized to contain the negative consequences of long-term psychological perturbation of the biological equilibrium leading to diabetic or CHD insults, etc. Thus, the brain may initiate or inhibit the inflammatory process; that is, it may activate the hypothalamus-pituitary-adrenal axis to induce APR where the parasympathetic nervous system mediates their detection by the central nervous system.

Although the animals used were rats raised and kept according to aseptic conditions, they reacted positively under various experimental conditions of psychological stimulation displaying different APR formats of neuroinflammation (tables 5 and 6) according to the intensity and frequency of applied psychological stimulus. In this context, the following two mechanistic alternatives are suggested to rationalize the observed psychosis-induced APR, namely,

(a) the neurological or psychological coding of the observed APR to external aggression threatening the model's physical existence is most likely *engraved* into rat's DNA mapping. Therefore, it is expected to be expressed at an opportune circumstance regardless of conditions of animal's breeding, and

(b) subjecting aseptically raised animals to *noise pollution* of cats' aggression is anticipated to decode an inflammatory sequence of events yielding the observed APR and organic injury.

Design of experimentations to characterize which of the two mechanistic routes above is predominantly contributing to the observed APR is feasible; however, it was not pursued further as it was not the main concern of our hypotheses. At this point, it is safe to assume: post-termination of the neurological or psychological stimulus, e.g., fear, dogmatic, etc., the amygdala remains electrophysiologically active. Repeated and timely dogmatic stimulation of the amygdala would trigger violence directed at a well-established target by these sermons. Medical injury in this area triggers violence as well. For example, two incidents—(a) the 1981 assassination of Sadat and (b) the 1961 massacre of 14 and the wounding of 38 individuals at the University of Texas by C. Whitman—best illustrate the induction of violence in response to dogmatic coaching and tumor growth in the vicinity of the amygdala respectively. Indeed, a postmortem autopsy of C. Whitman's brain revealed a glioblastoma multiforme tumor the size of a walnut compressing the amygdaloid nucleus. The educated extrapolation is, regardless of dogmatic or tumor activation, the electrophysiologically activated amygdala is expected to precipitate the release of a characteristic hepatic APR protein pattern into circulation.

Most recently, X-ray examination of brains of violent killers, rapists and robbers by Dr. Gerhard Roth, a professor at the University of Bremen (http://www.ifh.uni-bremen.de/roth/eindex.html), revealed a "dark patch" in the center of the brain denoted the evil spot where evilness lurks. A dark mass at the front of the brain appeared in all scans of people with violent criminal records. The assumption *"some criminals have a 'genetic predisposition' to violence"* supports our deduction: *the ethics and characteristics of violence could be hereditary features that are recessed in innocent offspring to materialize whenever necessary.* Furthermore, Dr. Ruth concluded: *criminal mental decline "begins in the kindergarten", but a positive parental environment and strong societal support can easily stop the child going on to offend. Equally, a negative domestic situation could easily lead to a child otherwise moderately pre-disposed to violence, to become a hardened criminal.*

A la our experimental procedure of stress-induced APR in rat model, criminals had their brain activity measured after seeing short films embracing brutal and squalid scenes; the small section at the front of their brains showed no emotions to violent scenes; i.e., it remained "dark". As well, areas of the brain where compassion and sorrow are evoked remained unchanged. To sum it, this most interesting study agrees with our conclusions above. Nonetheless, the valuable conclusion of Prof. Roth justifies basic research in animal model to quench the following quires:

1- Could rearing innocent young on the ethics and values of aggression induce the formation of the evil dark mass at the front of the brain?

2- Is the evil dark mass a permanent phenomenon? Is it reversible? Assuming the cessation of the aggressive stimulation, could psychotherapists eliminate the evil trend from adult criminals targeting given groups? If yes; could a rehabilitated criminal turn into committing the same very crimes?

3- Is the biology of formation and/or elimination (if possible) of evil-dark mass proportionally associated with chemical changes in the spectrum of serum proteins. Specifically triacylglycerols in terms of GLC-spectral abundance and elution pattern of a particularly extracted lipid sample?

4- It would be most beneficial to consider the X-ray protocol developed by Professor Roth to elaborate, if possible, on the genesis of the newly developing radical psychological-mental aberrations in terms of "dark, evil sex patch" in the following categories: (a) male aggressive sex drive and/or fear of rejection metamorphosed into necrophilia (mating with deceased wives) and pedophilia (marriage of elderly males to six- to seven-year-old female infants); (b) passion / mental state of young battered females to indiscriminately *breastfeed* (nurse) adult males under the pretext of budding brotherly bondage as a safeguard against possibilities of eventual fornications with peers;[*1] and (c) a combination of disadvantaged economics, aggressive reaction of some women and resignation[*2] of many

---

[*1] Most of the aggressive behavior of Middle Eastern females, incarcerated to male's dogmatic narcissism and chauvinistic whims, is covert. Therefore, their dominant model of response to stress is "tend and befriend" *versus* the typical males' "Fight or flight", i.e., *breast-feeding* adult males and jihad mating to accommodate the desires of the mujahedeen.

[*2] Does X-ray brain scanning of females with these particular attitudes of resignation or passivity show characteristic brain patch *a la* aggressive individuals?

to the humiliation of the societal-theocratic downgrading of females, may be the factors propelling the eccentric phenomenon of female drive into jihad-mating to accommodate the sexual urges of the mujahideen. According to official Tunisian statistics, on average, the outcome of a sexual tour of duty (http://www.liveleak.com/view?i=a77_1379726921&comments=1) a female could mate with approximately one hundred males. As a result of multiple mating with various Syrian mujahideen, many Tunisian females were impregnated. It is our contention; this cooperative impregnations would hasten the societal characterization of the unknown-father-born infants as the product of mother's agreeable multiple prostitution in Syria. More urgent is, entertaining the lack of hygiene and utter filth of their biome. Regardless of the mental aberrations of these females waging jihad-mating, they are a perfect crucible for the possible mutation of venereal diseases to *de-novo* insults. Intense emotion of loathing intermingled with violence is a common thread-factor that is equally and exclusively shared in-between these three categories that plagued Egypt post the brief Obama-tailored theocracy of Mursi.

http://new.elfagr.org/Detail.aspx?nwsId=427965&secid=1&vid=2

As a prelude to possible remedy, it would be mandatory to quantitate these anomalies in terms of plotting the intensity of the "dark, evil sex patch" against an agreed definition of the perturbation factor impelling said psychological injuries. Results of this medical research are more peaceful and much less expensive *vis-à-vis* spraying bullets in fields of war.[*3] If these lethal mental aberrations are left unattended by scientists, they are expected to inflict fatal injuries to the integrity of both inter- and intrahuman relations between individuals of both sexes in countries plagued with Obama's Arab Spring, viz., Egypt, Tunisia, Libya, Afghanistan, Syria, and Yemen. Furthermore, should these ghoulish characteristics be favored for the sake of a few barrels of crude oil and be allowed to nest and normalize within the ruined psyche of these dogmatic cults, it would firmly engrave their fingerprints within the milieu of the recently evolved Arab Spring states. Knowing the fabric of the Arab Spring nations is impregnated with poverty, ill education, extinct medical care, and radical vertical distribution of extracted wealth, etc., together with said psychological maladies, the Middle East would be an amenable recipe for a Malthusian anarchy and disaster.[5] That is, more lethal and perforating than the sarin gas, especially, the very many of these well-implanted dogmatic cults within the Europe and North America proper may play at tranquility at the moment but will show their canines at the opportune circumstance to have these aberrations exponentially flourishing within the boundaries of Western civilization.

Thus, it remains too early to decide if the genius of the thirty million Egyptian laypersons on June 30, 2013, has peacefully dismantled the threat of Obama's mental labor, the so-called Arab Spring. Egyptian Tamarod already juddered life into a popular unrest against the fundamentalists of Tunisia and the militants of Hamas. Aggression of said cults became a boundary-free fact of modern daily life. In his country of origin, Kenya, terrified shoppers huddled in back hallways and prayed they would not be found by the extremist gunmen lobbing grenades and firing assault rifles inside Nairobi's top mall on Saturday, September 21, 2013. Albeit the following extrapolation may sound implausible, it has a very particular merit to justify further experimentation. A link has been suggested between antisocial behavior and a defect in the gene that codes for monoamine oxidase A (MAO-A). Sluggish activity on the MAO-A gene results in a

---

[*3] The prestigious education at Harvard University together with the intellectual environment has amalgamated both JF Kennedy and RF Kennedy into Messianic and peaceful figures who advocated peace *versus* costly conflicts. The Peace Corps helped educating many third world individuals rather than recruiting them in vain wars.

substantial breakdown of neurotransmitters, such as serotonin. Serotonin is a rate determining human calmness. That is, a defect in serotonin may increase the urge to react aggressively to threats or fears (real or imaginary), leading MAO-A to be referred to as the "warrior" gene. The extrapolation is, *is there a quantitative relation between the "dark, evil sex patch" and the warrior gene?*

In the final analysis, Western multidisciplinary schemes embodying interwoven preventive medical and psychological parallels, redesigning the educational intake to distill morality into the current arid fabric of the Egyptian youth, rehabilitating ~8 million drug and dogmatic hallucinations-addicts, etc., are deemed essential. This is to peacefully salvage Egypt via democratic secularism and Western medical care according to the above proposed computer doctor. This is an ambitious approach to modernize Egypt, whose inhabitants are in long-term contact with environmental organic diseases and aggressively plagued with a unique array of societal characterization-induced maladies. For example, the MD chairman of the Physicians Union in Egypt, which supposedly embodies the most educated of the society, issued an absurd doctrinarian decree in the annals of medicine: "*Surgery involving organ transplants are subject to the dogmatic affiliations of the recipients and donors!*" By comparison, in Canada, at the Royal Victoria Hospital, Quebec, a team of surgeons bestowed life to a comatose patient with end-stage liver cirrhosis using a hog liver as an external tissue to filter toxins and reduce ammonia concentration in the patient's serum until a human donor liver was availed. Worse is the shuttling of a dogmatically-reared pompous professor of chemistry among cities of the area, whetting the verbose-anti-minorities bravado of the 1952 coup colonels among the dogmatically incited illiterates. The professors' coordinates are too consumed with childish emotional hate to palpate the worn-out fabric of present-day Egyptians in between the lice of poverty, ill-education, failing medical health, etc. Although the conceptualization and responsibilities associated with the notion "just society" are absolutely alien to the contemporary Egyptian population, a national daring scheme to detoxify the two already shrinking green stretches of the river Nile is an urgent task—that is, an obligatory ban on the use of herbicides, pesticides, and hormones in agriculture and animal husbandry while reverse-osmosis-desalinated water is consumed as an alternate source of potable water and for irrigation. This requires assembly of giant reverse osmosis units by the shores of the Mediterranean and the Red Sea. By definition, long-term irrigation with desalinated water will avail the opportunity to wash the banks of the river Nile, that is, to purge it of residual toxins.

Taking into consideration that Egypt is depicted as the gift of the Nile by the ancient Greek historian Herodotus, it is mandatory to reeducate current Egyptian farmers to respect and maintain the integrity of, and avoid intoxicating their source of life, the river Nile. A modern day echo to the philosophy of emperor Marcus Aurelius *"service and duty is to recognize and advocate equanimity in the midst of tribulations by following nature as a source of guidance and inspiration"* vibrated in the words of a notable political scholar, Robert Kennedy. He promised a working contract intellectually wrapped in few illuminating words: *"Some men see things as they are and say 'Why?' I dream things that never were and say 'Why not?'"* That was a promise to unleash the ingenuity of the youths to engage positively *vis-à-vis* the incessant, pounding *"Yes, we can!"* at the negative emotional resources of the working class. Alas, it evaporated rather rapidly, showing its true roots of shallowness. This intellectual poverty may prophesize the storming of the Western civilization by a dark age's avalanche according to the very many Middle Eastern recipes. It is safe to extrapolate the burning of the library of Alexandria by the nomads of AD 641 to the very same rituals that hatched the demolition of the World Trade Center 1,400 years later.

According to the wisdom *I dream things that never were and say 'Why not?'*, an agronomist and a food scientist member of the group carried out an explanatory experiment to produce organic food with minimal intoxications. The surface of a sandy area of 1600 m^2 60 Km to the city Alexandria was covered with 10 tons of the River Nile mud accumulated at the banks of Lake Nasser behind the high dam. The area was sprayed thrice daily with desalinated Mediterranean Sea water (reverse osmosis). Wide ranges of vegetation were planted. Animal manure was used as fertilizer. Excellent produce was obtained with very acceptable nutritional value and minimal toxic pollution. Unavoidably, the source of pollution is the animal manure. Data of these experimentations will be published in due course.

Sildenafil-Induced Hepatic Acute Phase Response

An animal model was developed to inquire into mechanisms of inhibition of libidinousness (unfulfillment) in sildenafil-addicted animals in terms of hepatic APR and behavioral irregularities. Egypt, in general and in particular Upper Egypt and the Nile delta villages, is a typical muscular male dominated society, (viz., recent legalization of Necrophilia between males and deceased wives). Alas, at this point of time, chauvinistic men supremacy is contradicted by toxins-induced male feminization. Incapacitated and bruised male pride together with fear of female sexuality, societal inhibitions and taboos and the common delusion, among Egyptians, of excessive intake of large doses of a medication for the purpose of prompt ameliorations of ailments, drove Egyptian males into addiction to sildenafil. Thus, it became essential to inquire into the side effects of addiction to sildenafil in animal model. Collected semen samples of Egyptian males with established infertility, 2408 individuals 18-47y, were examined. In general total volume of semen was less than 1ml, and the total number of spermatozoa per ejaculate was less than a million. The 10-27% alive spermatozoa were disfigured, i.e., low grade quality, as well sluggishly moving. According to our preliminary statistics, an unexpected 1.4-fold higher infertility was observed in Egyptian males, 18-47y, addicted to sildenafil. Therefore, we tailored dosages of sildenafil per Kg of our 30-days experimental animal model to approximate a 30-years excessive male addiction. Data of range of application of sildenafil per Kg male rabbits were assayed. The most acceptable results pertained to oral intubation of 30mg sildenafil per Kg rabbit. Sildenafil was orally administered to two same-sex animals of equal or different weights housed in the same cage. On day 2, male rabbits showed obvious arousal, hardening of the penis, and on day 5, ~20% of the heavier individuals became aggressively dominant and attempted mating with the smaller, turned passive male.

Initially, in comparison with the control group, a male pair weighing 2 kg±100 g per cage, sildenafil-treated animals gained weight, and 15% ejaculated 18 hours post day 4. As of day 8, animals lost ~20-30% weight concomitant with eccentric aggression, suggesting the channeling of repressed energy from a sexual-instinctive biological compartment into psychological aberrations. Energy channeling is proposed to maintain the animal at its lowest possible levels of energy necessary for the viability of other organs.

Ultimately, the mechanism hypothalamus (TRH) $\rightarrow$ pituitary (TSH) $\rightarrow$ thyroid (T4 and T3) was disrupted, leading to defective thyroid hormonal production, that is, decreased libido as a result of hypothyroidism. Therefore, it is safe to assume that sildenafil has cannibalized most of animals' pool of energy responsible for sustaining other biological functions into a sex-instinctual compartment. Consequently, excessive waste of skeletal muscle was inevitable to maintain the energy level of various compartments at near-ground-state levels. Female rabbits receiving sildenafil continued to gain weight and sporadically approached one another. Streptozotocin-diabetic male rabbits showed neither the symptoms of weight variations nor the sexual gestures to passive rabbits said above. However, they expired as of the 2nd week of the experiment.

Introduction

Most likely, penile erection is a synchronization of hormonal and neurovascular events modulated by a spectrum embracing the psyche of family values, societal and religious dictates, etc. Thus, erectile dysfunction (ED) could be defined as the optimization of psychogenic, arteriogenic, neurogenic, and endocrinologic factors; and the most common, neurogenic ED, may be the outcome of a deficiency of specific neurotransmitters.[27, 28] In general, sexuality is proportional to aging, health status, personal experience, interpersonal relationships, unique attitudes of partners, etc. Thus, a failing of one or more of these factors may lead to ED. In general, ED-diabetic, impotent males portrayed chronic SD *vis-à-vis* nondiabetic patients. Initially, diabetics responded well to ED treatment, but the improved response did not last for significant periods of time. Thus, it is highly recommended to medical doctors to provide long-term follow-up of ED in diabetics since it has greater impact on their emotional life.[29]

Sildenafil citrate was found to be a suitable oral therapy addressing the organic cause of ED. Release of nitric oxide (NO) in the corpus cavernosum during sexual stimulation is suggested to initiate the sequence of erection, that is, the activation of guanylate cyclase and the increase in the level of cyclic *cGMP*, thus inducing smooth muscle relaxation in the corpus cavernosum and subsequent increase in inflow of blood. In this context, sildenafil has no direct relaxant effect on isolated human corpus cavernosum but enhances the effect of NO by inhibiting *PDE5*, which is responsible for the degradation of *cGMP;* that is, sildenafil is ineffective in the absence of sexual stimulation. On the other hand, mechanisms of female sexuality and arousal are incompletely understood but are likely the composite of a complex interaction among the autonomic nervous system, sex hormones (e.g., estrogen and testosterone), and environmental factors encompassing mental health, fatigue, and quality of relationship with the partner. Thus, when evaluating and planning treatment of reduced sexual desire in women, this broad range of factors should be entertained. Sildenafil increases genital blood flow but may not impact on subjective reports of arousal.[30] However, recent reports suggest that:

(i) women taking sildenafil described increased vaginal blood flow, enhanced clitoral responsiveness, and increased lubrication[31], and

(ii) 9 of 10 females, 18-60 years old, recruited from a psychiatry clinic with SD (e.g., anorgasmia, loss of libido, and lubrication difficulties), but excluding individuals with diabetes mellitus, neurological disorders, genital anatomical defects, myocardial infarction, and alcoholism, reported a complete, or at least a significant, reversal of their SD.[32]

In a related study on animal models, vardenafil 1 mg kg[-1] was IV administered into sexually mature (~12 months old) female beagle dogs to assess changes in PNES-induced blood flow into the vagina and the clitoris. Said administration of vardenafil significantly potentiated the increases in blood flow into the vagina and the clitoris during the sexual arousal phase.[32] Thus, enhanced capillary permeability in females promotes a neurogenic transudate, leading to vaginal lubrication. Therefore, blood flow into the vagina and the clitoris, a measurable physiological response to sexual stimulation, is empirical for the study and the understanding of female sexuality. Furthermore, in the Egyptian male milieu, malignant with dogmatic downgrading of women, prevalent male feminization, and a wide spectrum of taboos and rituals, both sexes, particularly those of advanced age, or the young and affluent, are addicted to smuggled sildenafil. Nonetheless, deprived of sexual satisfaction. Accordingly, the consequences have crossed the boundaries of managing health ills into the pool of social tribulations. In the final analyses, considering addiction to sildenafil together with absence of viable programs of sex education, and abundance of taboos prohibiting the natural instinctive outcome to sexual stimulation, it is our contention: the experimental animal model of current presentation best describes the side effects of unfulfilled sexual desires in sildenafil-addicted individuals. The animal model was designed to report on induced hepatic APR and behavioral-psychological demeanor to addiction to sildenafil. According to present data, we are suggesting:

(i) acute unfulfilled sexuality in sildenafil-addicted male rabbits impelled sexual approach to passive animals, tunneling of the unfulfilled sexual energy, and libidinousness to yield aggression followed by loss of weight and general activity;

(ii) 30-day administration of sildenafil into a female rabbit model resulted in an obvious gain in weight, hepatic ARR, and sporadic attempts to mate with same-sex individuals; and

(iii) diabetic rabbits did not respond similarly to repeated sildenafil doses.

Three animal models were developed:

Oral Administration of Sildenafil into Healthy Rabbits and Housing of Animals: Animals were freely allowed water and an ad libitum rabbit chow diet. Two healthy male or female animals weighing ~2 kg were housed per cage. In another set of experiments, a ~2 kg male animal was housed with a ~1 kg same-sex rabbit. Sildenafil dose of 30 mg kg^{-1} was orally administered at 8:00 a.m. on a daily basis to all animals.

Oral Administration of Sildenafil into Diabetic Rabbits: 24-hour fasting rabbits became diabetic via introduction of streptozotocin (65 mg kg^{-1} body weight, in citrate buffer at pH 4.0) into their circulation. Sildenafil was orally administered into diabetic rabbits according to the protocol described above.

Oral Administration of Sildenafil into Snake Venom-Intoxicated Rabbits: Sildenafil 30 mg kg^{-1} was orally administered at 8:00 a.m. on a daily basis to rabbits intoxicated with cobra venom.

Discussion

Sildenafil-Addiction Model: Experimental conditions were tailored to inquire into sildenafil-induced hepatic APR and behavioral aberrations in animals coerced to negative dissipation synthesized by long periods of erection in response to initial libidinousness. The design and the purpose of the current scheme of experimentations negated animal anesthesia at any stage of the experiment, lest it may compromise the quantitative expression of hepatic APR to the administered drug and could dilute the psychological response of experimentally addicted animals to sildenafil. This was accomplished by housing two ~2 kg female or male rabbits per cage, and in another set of experiments, a ~2 kg animal shared the same cage with a same-sex rabbit, 1kg±200g. Sildenafil 30 mg Kg^{-1} was orally administered on a daily basis for 30 days. On day 2, male rabbits showed obvious hardening of the penis together with noticeable redness and enlargement of the testis, indicative of prior arousal. However, as of day 5, ~20% showed intermale aggression to mate with the second less-weight animal, which turned into a passive sex object with bluish testis 60% smaller by volume. Histology of the reduced-size bluish testis of passive rabbits documented complete spermatogenic arrest, that is, atrophy, possible feminization? Surprisingly, a sildenafil-addicted male rabbit with obvious redness and enlargement of the testis failed to approach a female of equal weight when caged together for 15 days and, accordingly, did not react as expected to addiction to sildenafil. This odd phenomenon may suggest that long-term breeding of siblings may yield offspring with unknown atrophied capabilities of some function(s) that dictate failure of sexual arousal. Besides pollution-induced feminization of Egyptian males, this observation may rationalize the failure of high proportions of the newly married young Egyptian couples to breed, inasmuch as >27-35% of them, according to geographical location, are the product of a long line of arranged first-cousin marriages, consanguinity?

Female rabbits sporadically approached one another, but not as aggressively as dominant males approached passive male rabbits. 15% of male rabbits ejaculated 18 hours post administration of sildenafil on day 4. Initially males gained weight; however, as of day 8 they had lost 20-30% weight, which may suggest emaciation of the psychic energy of the sex-instinctive biological drives.

According to the accepted theorem, the mechanism of male erection is contradicted by the PDE5-catalyzed degradation of *cGMP*. As sildenafil inhibits PDE5, enhancement of erection is anticipated. Accordingly, a hypothetical potential energy diagram (presentation 3) may approximate the present observation in the animal model. As in any chemical process, it is safe to theorize that both *cGMP* and PDE5 are in circulation and in equilibrium at different proportions that are determinants to the duration of erection; i.e., erection is subject to whichever of the two chemicals is in abundance. On attainment of ejaculation, PDE5 increases, leading to degradation of *cGMP* and reversal of erection so that the corresponding transition-state energy of the sexual drive assumes the ground state. Inhibition of PDE5 upon intake of sildenafil precipitates smooth muscle relaxation, but not necessarily ejaculation, which obliges continual availability of energy of activation $\Delta E2$ (presentation 3). Thus, it is safe to assume that sildenafil has routed most of animals' general pool of energy responsible for sustaining other biological functions into its sex-instinctual compartment. The most possible route is muscular degradation and lipolysis of adipose tissue leading to the observed muscle wasting and weight loss in the animal model. Excessive waste of skeletal muscle was inevitable to account for elevated free serum glucose and reduced cholesterol 1.5- and 0.4-fold *versus* healthy controls, respectively. On day 15 of the experiment, while exposed to the physical aggression of dominant male rabbits, ~35% and ~7% of passive males showed unilateral and total atrophy of the testis, respectively. On the other hand, female rabbits receiving sildenafil continued to gain weight.

For the survival of sildenafil-addicted animals, it is logical to assume that the biological order had to regain stability of the ground state, thus demoting the transitional-state sexual energy via tunneling into neurosis and/or behavioral aggression targeting the passive male. A ~7-10% of dominant male rabbits who failed this mechanism continued to gain weight to expire 7±2 days prior to the termination of the experiment. Passive male rabbits showed serum chemistry similar to that of sildenafil-addicted female rabbits, manifesting a typical multi-inflammatory hepatic APR due to wounds (e.g., stress inflected by dominant rabbits and possibly cardiac irregularities initiated by addiction to sildenafil). Histology of heart muscle and hepatic tissue of passive male rabbits showed severe degenerative-necrotic fibers and critical fatty accumulations in hepatocytes together with necroinflammatory foci respectively. At early stages (10-15 days) of forced addiction to sildenafil, histology documented that hepatic tissue was in a regenerative path, that is, hepatocytes with two nuclei. This is indicative of typical hepatic regeneration in response to necrosis induced by forced addiction of animals to sildenafil. Most likely, in passive male rabbits, the mechanism pertaining to

$$\text{hypothalamus (TRH)} \rightarrow \text{pituitary (TSH)} \rightarrow$$
$$\text{thyroid (T4 and T3)} \rightarrow \text{increased metabolism}$$

was disrupted, leading to defective thyroid hormonal production, that is, decreased libido as a result of hypothyroidism. Histology of the visually reddish and large testis of the dominant individuals revealed partial spermatogenic arrest suggesting necrosis of sperms at the location of their incipience. This is most likely due to either (a) accumulated stress of retaining seminal fluid without periodic discharge and/or (b) sildenafil and/or metabolite-induced toxicity. In this context, it is inescapable to comment on the evolutionary process, which is assumed to have flawlessly attained its purpose of a perfect man/woman as the end product. For the preservation of species, in healthy males, sperms are biosynthesized and released at any time regardless of the male's age, while females are born with a specific number of ova, which are released once per month, and their biology deteriorates in advanced-age females with concomitant risks of delivering genetically deformed infants. Therefore, it is acceptable to entertain the hypothesis pertaining to males' having reached their optimal evolution and are most likely declining. The fragility of males' reproductive machinery is evident as it deteriorates upon exposure to environmental toxins (e.g., pesticides, mycotoxins, etc). As every new life is a mutation of the previous, unless it is a perfect clone, it is feasible to suggest that the female gender is possibly in evolution to the immaculate ideal of releasing an ovum whenever mating is necessary, *versus* the menstrual cycle to ovulate a predetermined number of ova. Thus, it saves energy expenditure required to rebuild the endometrium every fertility cycle and minimizes the vulnerability of the ova's chromatin to problems of division and breakage. Eventually, fetuses and infants of older mothers would have lesser probabilities of chromosomal abnormalities. This hypothetical female mutation increases the possibility of continuation of our species with greater chances of survival and/or adaptation to the current unfavorable intoxication of environment.

We are documenting the vulnerability of diabetic rabbits to sildenafil-induced addiction; most of experimental animals expired on the 15-18th days of the experiment with concomitant accumulation of PF proportional to hepatic necrosis. Histology suggested earlier sildenafil-induced damage to hepatic and cardiac tissues of diabetic rabbits *vis-à-vis* healthy animals. Histology of hepatic tissue on the 4th day of addiction revealed the presence of double nuclear hepatocytes, suggesting early hepatic regeneration to necrosis. Under these experimental conditions, remaining viable hepatocytes reacted to multi-inflammatory stimulations (e.g., hepatic and cardiac cellular necrosis, cardiac irregularities, stress, sildenafil, and/or metabolites intoxication) by releasing higher concentrations of APR proteins. This would further multiply chances of cardiac anomalies, leading to the observed early expiry of experimental sildenafil-addicted diabetic animals. Furthermore, post 3rd day of addiction to sildenafil, dominant diabetic male rabbits expressed neither aggressive behavior, initial gain of weight, nor sexual advances to the passive individual as *vis-à-vis* addicted controls. Both dominant and diabetic passive males addicted to sildenafil continued to lose weight until expiry. In all models, liver enzymes ALT and AST were elevated during the course of the experiment, indicative of hepatic inflammation and necrosis. Addiction of cobra-intoxicated rabbits to sildenafil induced a behavioral and weight-loss pattern similar to that of healthy individuals, except with 30% increase in PF.

Sildenafil-Induced APR Model

As expected, an orally administered single dose of sildenafil to singularly caged male and/or female rabbits evoked an orthodox inflammatory APR to induced hepatic necrosis provoked by the drug or its metabolites. In the male rabbit model, day 1 post administration of a single dose, relative concentrations of pre-Alb, Alb, and TF decreased by -19, -12, and -9, while AGP, At, Hp, and C3 +C3c increased by +36, +26, +29 and +14%, respectively (table 7). It is noteworthy that identified APR proteins, except for At, regressed almost to healthy levels of healthy controls on the 9th day of the experiment. Elevated concentration of At is pivotal to the catabolism of excessive cellular debris, muscular and various intracellular proteins and glycoproteins to provide hepatic and other cellular compartments with monomeric carbohydrates and amino acids necessary for the regeneration and amelioration of sildenafil-induced cellular damage. Increased levels of ALT and AST were observed to last for the duration of the experiment (table 7), which confirms hepatocellular necrosis. On the other hand, synthetic addiction to sildenafil manifested an APR typical of a hepatic tissue plagued by multi-inflammatory stimuli. That is, under the current set of coerced addiction to sildenafil, combined neurotic, cardiac, testicular, etc., lesions evoked a mute APR as of the 3rd day of the experiment together with unyielding high concentrations of serums' ALT and AST until the 30th day of the experiment or the expiry of animals.

In streptozotocin-induced diabetes in rabbits, relative concentration of pre-Alb, Alb, TF, AGP, At, Hp, and C3 +C3c decreased -72, -23, -35, -16, -7, -22, and -35% respectively *vis-à-vis* healthy controls. Even though diabetes promotes vascular dysfunction, hypertension, and deranged hepatic mechanisms in experimental animals, addiction to sildenafil induced a particular profile of inflammatory APR. Contrary to the orthodoxy of hepatic inflammatory response, diabetic male rabbits addicted to sildenafil showed a moderate 5th-day elevation in concentrations of above-said APR proteins to -37, -9, -15, -10, -3, -6, and -23% respectively. Most likely, this increase in the percentage of APR proteins is a biological avenue to deplete circulation of excess glucose via the biosynthesis and the release-elevated concentrations of APR proteins necessary to initiate and to maintain cellular recovery post intoxication. Nonetheless, on day 15, the relative concentrations of APR proteins decreased to parallel percentages of diabetic animal control, ND, -24, -22, -18, -9, -11, and -23 respectively. This may be indicative of inefficient organic function of the liver to withstand maintaining its biological tasks, thus precipitating the early expiry of the animal model. Accumulation of PF in the diabetic animal model may imply acute hepatic inflammation and necrosis induced by addiction to sildenafil. The fragility of this animal model suggests extreme care should be exercised when prescribing sildenafil to diabetic patients. On the other hand, the spectrum of APR of cobra-intoxicated rabbits to sildenafil was typical of a hepatic response to multi-inflammatory stimuli. According to present data, in all models whenever possible to collect PF, CSF, and SF, all showed the same serum chemistry and inflammatory 2D-IEP spectrum parallel to that of corresponding serum proteins.

In the final analysis, it is safe to assume that we are living in the age of many contradictory and/or conflicting drug interactions with many animal organs having different functionalities; that is, chemicals developed to medically manage specific ailments could be favorably applied to contain other pathologies. In this context, considering (a) sildenafil displayed a general smooth muscle relaxation, thus precipitating a long-term inflow of blood within the smooth muscle, and (b) mechanisms involving mediation by LEM and interleukins were postulated earlier to account for the release of ascetic fluids into the peritoneal cavity of cholera-intoxicated aseptic and diabetic rat models, it is a logical anticipation to assume oral intake of sildenafil may facilitate accumulation of ascetic fluids in certain events of intoxication. Our preliminary observations suggest that sildenafil enhanced by ~30% the extra inflow of ascetic fluids embracing APR proteins in male rabbits intoxicated with cobra venom (0.1 mg Kg^{-1} body weight). Therefore, we are suggesting that under specific conditions of administration, the basic biological functionality of sildenafil may warrant its efficacy as an anti-inflammatory agent to certain insults. This assumption must be elaborated on by detailed and intensive basic research.

Table 1. Statistical Distribution of HCV among Egyptian Major Cities and Regions

Location	Prevalence	Population	No. infected
Alexandria	5.9	4,668,870	275,463
Cairo	8.2	15,226,140	1,248,543
Lower Egypt	28.4	33,390,476	9,482,895
Middle Egypt	26.5	18,223,122	4,829,127
Upper Egypt	19.4	8,826,429	1,712,327
TOTALS	21.8	80,335,036	17,548,356

Table 2. Serum, Sperm, and Colostrum Samples Analyses

	HCV	HBV	*HBP*	Malaria	α-FP	HDV	HGV
Males Serum (217)	27	4	192	197	196	4	2
Semen of HCV (17)	11						
Semen of HBV (4)		1					
Female Serum (32)	6	-ve	26	25	25		
Pregnant females (10)	4	-ve	8	8	9		
Colostrum of HCV Females (4)	2						

J.H. WASSILI AND CYRIL BARADAEUS

Table 3. % Contraction of Tested Pathogens in Serum of Female (F) and Male (M) Individuals.

	M tested			F tested		
	(>20-60y, 1*)	(>10-20y, 0.37*)	(<10y, 0.45*)	(>20-60y, 1*)	(>10-20y, 0.57*)	(<10y, 1.14*)
HBP	44	50.4	30	88	72	61
HCV	23	0	0	38	16.7	11
HBV	2.1	14.4	5	6.3	1.6	5.6
α-FP	92	73	81	95	83	88
Malaria	90	91	96	95	91	92
Glu*	-30 ± 7	-35 ± 6	-25 ± 10	-27 ± 4	-28 ± 5	-34 ± 7
CHO*	-19 ± 4	-24 ± 5	-35 ± 8	-17 ± 4	-23 ± 6	-31 ± 4
TG*	-23 ± 8	-28 ± 6	-31 ± 7	-15 ± 2	-21 ± 4	-32 ± 6

*Entries are percentages of decrease of Glu, CHO and TG relative to same age group of healthy Canadian individuals.

Table 4. Percent Changes in Plasma Proteins of (a) HCV Renal Failure Patients and (b) Animal Immune Rejection Model in Serum and Peritoneal Fluid Relative to Healthy Individuals

Body fluid	TP	Alb	AGP	Pre-Alb	Hp	CRP	Fb	TF	At	CHO	Glu	ALT	AST	UA	Urea	TG
Human serum	-60	-67	-25	-85	-27	-27	-8	-51	-11	-15	-9	+3	+5	+3	+6	-11
Human peritoneal fluid	-64	-69	-34	ND	-35	-41	-12	-43	-23	-21	-12	-2	-5	-5	-1	-19
Human serumVD	-48	-52	-12	-80	-22	-24	-5	-41	-7	-18	-11	+4	+6	-5	-3	-5
Rabbits serum	-42	-53	-21	ND	-15	-21	-5	-15	-9	+5	-4	+15	+67	+12	+18	+3
Rabbits peritoneal fluid	-50	-59	-19	ND	-20	-20	-17	-23	-10	+2	-8	+25	+35	+9	+2	+8

Entries are the average of 4 determinations for body fluids of 56 end-stage HCV patients coupled with renal failure necessitating kidney dialysis and the average of 5 determinations of 12 animals undergoing hepatic rejection. Human serumVD denotes human serum of end-stage HCV and renal failure patients subsisted 30d on vegetarian diets. Uncertainty in above values ranged between +6-17% in immunoelectrophoretic and +2-5% in wet chemistry data. (ND denotes "not detectable.")

Table 5. Percent Change in Area of Immunoprecipitate APR Protein to Healthy Control Induced by Unscheduled Psychological Stress in (a) Daylight and (b) Darkness of Night

	a				b			
APR Protein	1d	3d	7d	15d	1d	3d	7d	15d
AGP	63	234	189	153	99	290	201	145
Hg	21	36	18	12	27	45	27	15
Fb	90	150	111	81	111	189	120	72
α-At	51	72	72	42	63	108	102	33
Alb	-9	-15	-18	-15	-8	-15	-14	-14
Pre-Alb	-8	-12	-15	-9	-8	-9	-11	-15
Glucose	1.04	1.07	1.16	1.20	1.06	1.12	1.16	1.22

Table 6. Percent Change in Area of Immunoprecipitate APR Protein to Healthy Control Induced by Scheduled Psychological Stress in Daylight

APR Protein	1d	3d	7d	15d
AGP	72	183	129	63
Hg	24	33	15	15
Fb	92	120	91	63
α-At	54	63	51	42
Alb	-10	-10	-15	-12
Pre-Alb	-7	-15	-11	-12
Glucose	1.04	1.08	1.19	1.15

Table 7. Experimental coordinates of healthy and diabetic animal models' addiction to sildenafil.

Experiment	Alb	Pre-Alb	TF	AGP	At	Hp	C3+C3c	ALT U/L	AST U/L
Sildenafil-SD-Control d1	-12	-19	-9	+36	+26	+29	+14	50.8	31.7
Sildenafil-SD-Control d3	-8	-29	-4	+18	+42	+ 7	+ 9	51.9	35.9
Sildenafil-SD-Control d5	-5	-23	-7	+18	+39	+12	+ 5	48.8	36.4
Sildenafil-SD-Control d9	-1	-7	-4	+ 3	+40	+ 5	+ 2	44.7	30.9
Sildenafil-Adic-Control d3	-12	-25	-15	+ 9	+21	+18	+ 9	57.2	37.1
Sildenafil-Adic-Control d5	-17	-34	-21	+10	+19	+12	+12	60.0	40.2
Sildenafil-Adic-Control d9	-23	-35	-19	+18	+23	+ 9	+21	58.6	39.9
Sildenafil-Adic-Control d15	-25	-45	-27	+25	+18	+ 5	+ 8	63.5	45.7
Sildenafil-Adic-Control d21	-23	-65	-25	+11	+ 9	-5	-6	61.2	44.9
Sildenafil-Adic-Control d30	-31	ND	-30	+ 5	+ 3	-13	-12	63.0	46.8
Diabetic-control D9	-23	-72	-35	-16	-7	-22	-35	43.3	27.9
Sildenafil-Adic-Diabetic d2	-11	-45	-30	-8	-7	-11	-30	59.1	43.3
Sildenafil-Adic-Diabetic d5	-9	-37	-15	-10	-3	-6	-23	60.0	43.4
Sildenafil-Adic-Diabetic d8	-5	-21	-9	-14	+ 6	-3	-16	59.4	40.5
Sildenafil-Adic-Diabetic d15	-24	ND	-22	-18	-9	-11	-23	58.2	39.6
Average uncertainty	±6	±10	±8	±12	±11	±9	±12	±7	±6

Sildenafil single dose control (Sildenafil-SD-Control), sildenafil-addicted control (Sildenafil-Adic-Control); sildenafil-addicted diabetic model (Sildenafil-Adic-Diabetic); and Not Detectable (ND). For the duration of experiment, average values of ALT and AST in serum of healthy animals were 41.3 and 25.8 U/L respectively. Estimates of percent changes in relative concentrations of APR serum proteins, ALT, and AST are the average of three determinations.

Scheme 1

Chemical and viral-induced hepatic inflammation $\longrightarrow$ LEM and IL-6 $\longrightarrow$ release of APR plasma proteins into peritoneum cavity $\longrightarrow$ Persistent inflammation (Long term APR) $\longrightarrow$ hepatic necrosis $\longrightarrow$ Hepatopoietin-induced hepatic regeneration $\longrightarrow$ increased liver mass

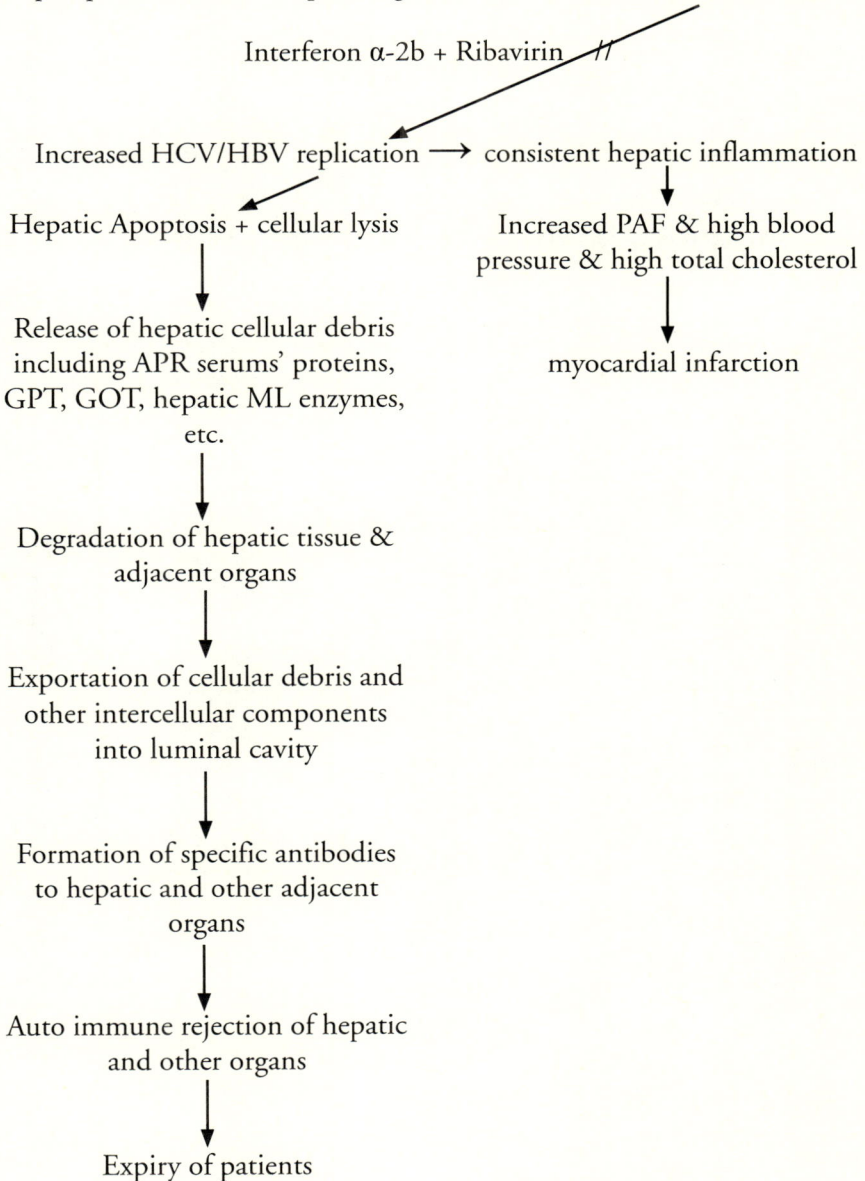

Interferon α-2b + Ribavirin ⫽

Increased HCV/HBV replication $\longrightarrow$ consistent hepatic inflammation

Hepatic Apoptosis + cellular lysis   Increased PAF & high blood pressure & high total cholesterol

Release of hepatic cellular debris including APR serums' proteins, GPT, GOT, hepatic ML enzymes, etc.   myocardial infarction

Degradation of hepatic tissue & adjacent organs

Exportation of cellular debris and other intercellular components into luminal cavity

Formation of specific antibodies to hepatic and other adjacent organs

Auto immune rejection of hepatic and other organs

Expiry of patients

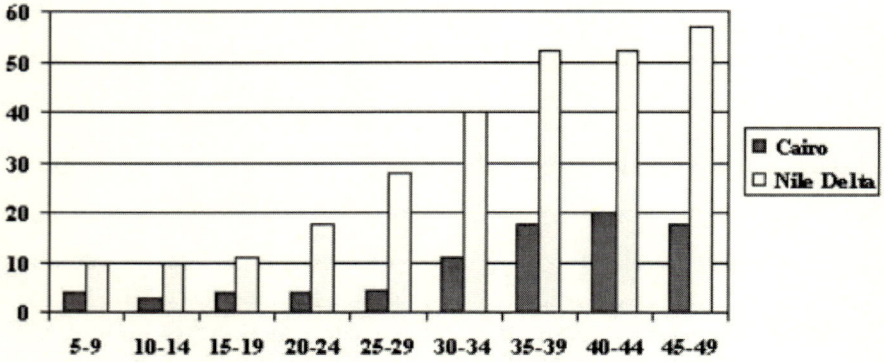

Presentation 1: <http://www.hepegypt.org/hep_in_egypt/hep.htm>

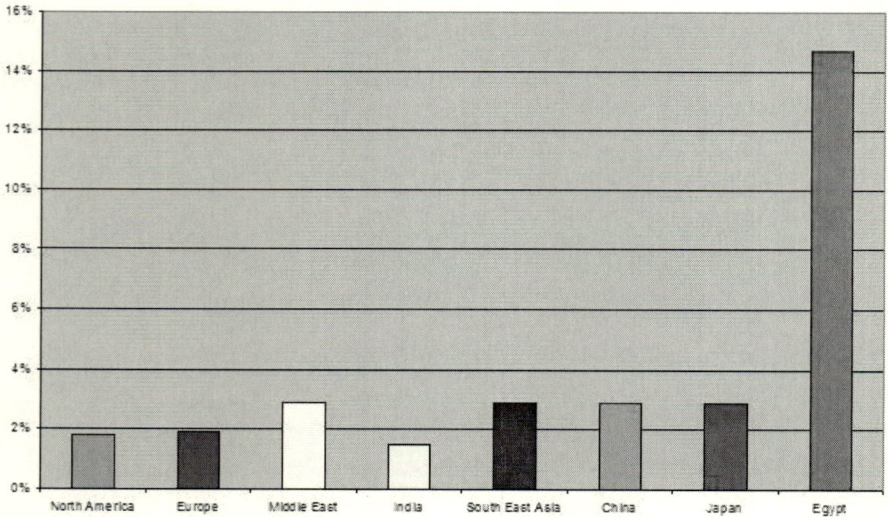

Presentation 2: http://www2.hawaii.edu/~dewolfe/Epidemic.html

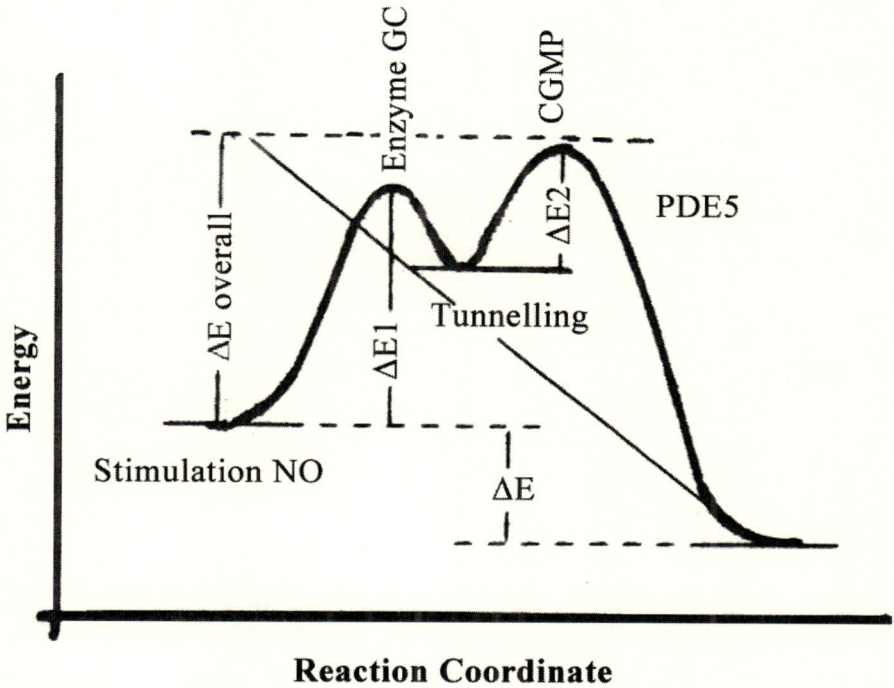

Presentation 3: Sildenafil, a Hypothetical Potential Energy Diagram

References

1. *Al Messa,* March 12, **2005**, March 1 and April 6, **2007**; *Al-Gomhuria,* March 1, **2009**; *Al-Masry Al-Youm,* September 29, **2006**; May 28-29, **2008**.
2. *Ad-Dustour,* May 13 and June 15, **2008**.
3. *Rose al-Yousef,* June 11, **2007**.
4. *Al-Masry Al-Youm,* May 8, **2008**.
5. Martin Donohoe, "Causes and Health Consequences of Environmental Degradation and Social Injustice," *Social Science and Medicine* 56 (**2003**): 573-87; and Thomas Robert Malthus, *An Essay on the Principle of Population* (**1798**), *http://www.docstoc.com/docs/6104911/Malthusian_catastrophe.*
6. John F. Risher, Franklin L. Mink, and Jerry F. Stara, "The Toxicologic Effects of the Carbamate Insecticide Aldicarb in Mammals: A Review," *Environmental Health Perspectives* 72 (**1987**): 267-81.
7. Gavin L. Meerdink, "Organophosphorus and Carbamate Insecticide Poisoning in Large Animals," *Veterinary Clinics of North America: Food Animal Practice* 5 (**1989**): 375-89.
8. Christoph Neumann-Haefelin, Hubert E. Blum, Frank V. Chisari, and Robert Thimme, "T Cell Response in Hepatitis C Virus Infection," *Journal of Clinical Virology* 32 (**2005**): 75-85.
9. Erica M. C. D'Agata, et al., "Modelling the Invasion of Community-Acquired Methicillin-Resistant *Staphylococcus aureus* into the Hospital Setting," *Clinical Infectious Diseases* 48 (**2009**): 274-84 and references therein.
10. Yvan J. F. Hutin, et al., "An Outbreak of Hospital-Acquired Hepatitis B Virus Infection among Patients Receiving Chronic Hemodialysis," *Infection Control and Hospital Epidemiology* 20 (**1999**): 731-35.

11. *http://afp.google.com/article/ALeqM5jzfJENPjPahpCoQhtRUCa K2O2YpQ*

12. Dong Jin Suh and Sook-Hyang Jeong, "Current Status of Hepatitis C Virus Infection in Korea," *Intervirology* 49 (**2006**): 70-5.

13. Anuradha Budhu and Xin Wei Wang, "The Role of Cytokines in Hepatocellular Carcinoma," *Journal of Leukocyte Biology* 80 *(**2006**)*: 1197-213.

14. *Al-Maydan*, April 25, **2007**.

15. Thea M. Edwards, Brandon C. Moore, and Louis J. Guillette Jr., "Reproductive Dysgenesis in Wildlife: A Comparative View," *International Journal of Andrology* 29 (**2006**): 109-21.

16. *Al-Masry Al-Youm,* May 18, **2006,** and June 14, **2008;** Rosa Al-Yousef, June 11, **2007**.

17. *www.newworldencyclopedia.org/entry/Amish#Religious_Practices_ and_Lifestyle;*   *www.researchgrantdatabase.com/g/1Z01HG000182/;* *www.masrawy.com/News/Egypt/Politics/2008/august/17/organs.aspx;* http://www.ahewar.org/debat/show.art.asp?aid=20231.

18. *UN Environmental Health Criteria* 64, International Program on Chemical Safety (Geneva, World Health Organization, **1986)** *http://www.inchem.org/documents/ehc/ehc/ehc64.htm#SubSection Number: 1.1.4.*

19. Oranan Prommano, et al., "A Quantitative Ultrastructural Study of the Liver and the Spleen in Fatal Falciparum Malaria," *Southeast Asian J Trop Med Public Health* 36 (**2005**): 1359-370.

20. Polrat Wilairatana Sornchai Looareesuwan, and Panta Charoenlarp, "Liver Profile Changes and Complications in Jaundiced Patients with Falciparum Malaria," *Trop Med Parasitol* 45 (**1994**): 298-330.

21. Alexander Neri, et al., "*Enterobius* (Oxyuris) *vermicularis* of the Pelvic Peritoneum—a Cause of Infertility," *European Journal of Obstetrics & Gynecology & Reproductive Biology* 23 (**1986**): 239-41.

22. Raj K. Singh, et al., "Prospective Analysis of the Association of Infection with CagA Bearing Strains of *Helicobacter pylori* and Coronary Heart Disease," *Heart* 88 (**2002**): 43-6; and Nicholas J. Wald, Malcolm R. Law, Joan K. Morris, Anne-Marie Bagnall, "*Helicobacter pylori* Infection and Mortality from Ischaemic Heart Disease: Negative Result from a Large, Prospective Study," *British Medical Journal* 315 (**1997**): 1199-1201.

23. Paul H. Black, "The Inflammatory Response Is an Integral Part
of the Stress Response: Implications for Atherosclerosis, Insulin
Resistance, Type-II Diabetes and Metabolic Syndrome X," *Brain,
Behavior and Immunity* 17 (**2003**): 350-64; Paul H. Black,
"Stress and the Inflammatory Response: A Review of Neurogenic
Inflammation," *Brain, Behavior and Immunity* 16 (**2002**): 622-53
and references therein.

24. Leanne M. Williams, et al., "Trauma Modulates Amygdala and Medial
Prefrontal Responses to Consciously Attended Fear," *Neuroimage*
29 (**2006**): 347-357; "Lesbian, Gay, Bisexual and Transgender
Youth: An Epidemic of Homelessness," *http://www.thetaskforce.
org/downloads/HomelessYouth.pdf*; "Understanding the Impact of
Trauma and Urban Poverty on Family Systems: Risks, Resilience,
and Interventions," *http://fittcenter.umaryland.edu/LinkClick.aspx?fi
leticket=jFOaDJRM1P8%3D&tabid=147*; "A Response to the God
Delusion," *http://sexton.clarityconnect.com/GodDelusionResponse.
pdf*; Samuel Pfeifer and Ursula Waelty, "Psychopathology and
Religious Commitment: A Controlled Study," *Psychopathology*
28 (**1995**): 70-77; Julie Rife and David Lester, "Religiosity and
Psychological Disturbance," *Psychological Reports* 81 (**1997**):
978; *Homelessness, Citizenship, and Identity, http://wxy.seu.edu.cn/
humanities/sociology/htmledit/uploadfile/system/20100723/
20100723182907849.pdf*; and *Neurobiology of Aggression,
ftp://195.214.211.1/books/DVD-022/Mattson_M.P._Neurobiology_
of_Aggression%5Bc%5D_Understanding_and_Preventing_Violence
_%282003%29%28en%29%28336s%29.pdf*

25. *http://bikyamasr.wordpress.com/2009/08/27/bm-womenreport-says-
sexual-harassment-in-egypt-staggering/*; *Al-Masri Al-Youm,* August
11, **2007,** reported a 13-year-old Egyptian girl has died during
an illegal operation to mutilate her genitalia; Nancy Mann Kulish,
"The Mental Representation of the Clitoris: The Fear of Female
Sexuality," *Psychoanalytic Inquiry* 11 (**1991**): 511-536.

26. Lyudmila V. Borovikova, et al., "Vagus Nerve Stimulation
Attenuates the Systemic Inflammatory Response to Endotoxin,"
Nature 405 (**2000**): 458-462; Claude Libert, "Inflammation: A
Nervous Connection," *Nature* 421 (**2003**): 328-329; and Andrej
A. Romanovsky, et al., "Fever and Hypothermia in Systemic

Inflammation: Recent Discoveries and Revisions," *Frontiers in Bioscience* 10 (**2005**): 2193-2216.

27. Gloria A. Bachman and Nancy A. Phillips, "*Sexual Dysfunction*," in *Chronic Pelvic Pain: An Integrated Approach*, John F. Steege, Deborah A. Metzger (Philadelphia: WB Saunders, **1998**), 77-90.

28. Tom F. Lue, "Neurogenic Erectile Dysfunction," *Clinical Autonomic Research* 11 (**2001**): 285-294.

29. David F. Penson, et al., "Do impotent men with diabetes have more severe erectile dysfunction and worse quality of life than the general population of impotent patients?" Results from the Exploratory Comprehensive Evaluation of Erectile Dysfunction (ExCEED) database, *Diabetes Care* 26 (**2003**): 1093-1099.

30. Cindy M. Meston and Penny F. Frohlich, "Update on Female Sexual Function," *Current Opinion on Urology* 11 (**2001**): 603-609.

31. I.D. Singer, "Patients Are Talking about Viagra," *Strategic Medicine* 2 (**1998**): 42-44.

32. H. George Nurnberg, et al., "Sildenafil for Sexual Dysfunction in Women Taking Antidepressants," *American Journal of Psychiatry* 156 (**1999**): 1664; and Javier Angulo, et al., "Vardenafil Enhances Clitoral and Vaginal Blood Flow Responses to Pelvic Nerve Stimulation in Female Dogs," *International Journal of Impotence Research* 15 (**2003**): 137-141.

Index

O

organs
   rejection of, 32-33, 70, 73
   transplantation of, 39-40, 56
Östersund, 12
ova, 16, 65

P

pathogens, mutation of, 11, 70
PDE5 (phosphodiestrase type 5), 64
pegylated interferon, 38-39
penile erection, 10, 60, 63-64
pinta. *See Treponema carateum*
proteins, 23-24, 31-34, 67-68
psychological stress
   scheduled, 49-50
   unscheduled, 50

R

renal failure, 22-23
ribavirin, 38-39

S

Schistosoma mansoni, 21
SD (sexual dysfunction), 61
sensory capacity, 13
sildenafil, 58-68, 72, 75, 80
Spanish influenza, 11
spermatogenic arrest, 65
surface-charge densities, 14
syphilis, 29

T

tetrapods, 15, 38
Thothrekh (son of an Egyptian high
   priest), 18
T. pertenue (*Treponema pertenue*), 29
transferrin, 10
Treponema carateum, 29
Treponema microdentium, 29
Treponema pallidum, 29
triacyl, 14

V

vardenafil, 61, 80
violence, 35
VMAT2 (vesicular monoamine
   transporter 2), 41

W

Whitman, C., 52

Y

yaws. *See T. pertenue*
   (*Treponema pertenue*)

Edwards Brothers Malloy
Thorofare, NJ USA
May 22, 2014